SCARECROW STUDIES IN YOUNG ADULT LITERATURE
Series Editor: Patty Campbell

Scarecrow Studies in Young Adult Literature is intended to continue the body of critical writing established in Twayne's Young Adult Authors Series and to expand it beyond single-author studies to explorations of genres, multicultural writing, and controversial issues in young adult (YA) reading. Many of the contributing authors of the series are among the leading scholars and critics of adolescent literature, and some are YA novelists themselves.

The series is shaped by its editor, Patty Campbell, who is a renowned authority in the field, with a thirty-year background as critic, lecturer, librarian, and teacher of YA literature. Patty Campbell was the 2001 winner of the ALAN Award, given by the Assembly on Adolescent Literature of the National Council of Teachers of English for distinguished contribution to YA literature. In 1989 she was the winner of the American Library Association's Grolier Award for distinguished service to young adults and reading.

1. *What's So Scary about R. L. Stine?* by Patrick Jones, 1998.
2. *Ann Rinaldi: Historian and Storyteller*, by Jeanne M. McGlinn, 2000.
3. *Norma Fox Mazer: A Writer's World*, by Arthea J. S. Reed, 2000.
4. *Exploding the Myths: The Truth about Teens and Reading*, by Marc Aronson, 2001.
5. *The Agony and the Eggplant: Daniel Pinkwater's Heroic Struggles in the Name of YA Literature*, by Walter Hogan, 2001.
6. *Caroline Cooney: Faith and Fiction*, by Pamela Sissi Carroll, 2001.
7. *Declarations of Independence: Empowered Girls in Young Adult Literature, 1990–2001*, by Joanne Brown and Nancy St. Clair, 2002.
8. *Lost Masterworks of Young Adult Literature*, by Connie S. Zitlow, 2002.
9. *Beyond the Pale: New Essays for a New Era*, by Marc Aronson, 2003.
10. *Orson Scott Card: Writer of the Terrible Choice*, by Edith S. Tyson, 2003.
11. *Jacqueline Woodson: "The Real Thing,"* by Lois Thomas Stover, 2003.
12. *Virginia Euwer Wolff: Capturing the Music of Young Voices*, by Suzanne Elizabeth Reid, 2003.

13. *More Than a Game: Sports Literature for Young Adults*, by Chris Crowe, 2004.
14. *Humor in Young Adult Literature: A Time to Laugh*, by Walter Hogan, 2005.
15. *Life Is Tough: Guys, Growing Up, and Young Adult Literature*, by Rachelle Lasky Bilz, 2004.
16. *Sarah Dessen: From Burritos to Box Office*, by Wendy J. Glenn, 2005.
17. *American Indian Themes in Young Adult Literature*, by Paulette F. Molin, 2005.
18. *The Heart Has Its Reasons: Young Adult Literature with Gay/Lesbian/Queer Content, 1969-2004*, by Michael Cart and Christine A. Jenkins, 2006.
19. *Karen Hesse*, by Rosemary Oliphant-Ingham, 2005.
20. *Graham Salisbury: Island Boy*, by David Macinnis Gill, 2005.
21. *The Distant Mirror: Reflections on Young Adult Historical Fiction*, by Joanne Brown and Nancy St. Clair, 2006.
22. *Sharon Creech: The Words We Choose to Say*, by Mary Ann Tighe, 2006.
23. *Angela Johnson: Poetic Prose*, by KaaVonia Hinton, 2006.
24. *David Almond: Memory and Magic*, by Don Latham, 2006.
25. *Aidan Chambers: Master Literary Choreographer*, by Betty Greenway, 2006.

Aidan Chambers

Master Literary Choreographer

Betty Greenway

*Scarecrow Studies in
Young Adult Literature, No. 25*

The Scarecrow Press, Inc.
Lanham, Maryland • Toronto • Oxford
2006

SCARECROW PRESS, INC.

Published in the United States of America
by Scarecrow Press, Inc.
A wholly owned subsidiary of
The Rowman & Littlefield Publishing Group, Inc.
4501 Forbes Boulevard, Suite 200, Lanham, Maryland 20706
www.scarecrowpress.com

PO Box 317
Oxford
OX2 9RU, UK

Copyright © 2006 by Betty Greenway

All rights reserved. No part of this publication may be reproduced, stored in a retrieval system, or transmitted in any form or by any means, electronic, mechanical, photocopying, recording, or otherwise, without the prior permission of the publisher.

British Library Cataloguing in Publication Information Available

Library of Congress Cataloging-in-Publication Data

Greenway, Betty.
  Aidan Chambers : master literary choreographer / Betty Greenway.
    p. cm. — (Scarecrow studies in young adult literature ; 25)
  Includes bibliographical references and index.
  ISBN-13: 978-0-8108-5087-3 (alk. paper)
  ISBN-10: 0-8108-5087-7 (alk. paper)
  1. Chambers, Aidan—Criticism and interpretation. 2. Young adult literature, English—History and criticism. I. Title. II. Series.
PR6053.H285Z67 2006
823'.914—dc22
                                                              2006008872

∞™ The paper used in this publication meets the minimum requirements of American National Standard for Information Sciences—Permanence of Paper for Printed Library Materials, ANSI/NISO Z39.48-1992.
Manufactured in the United States of America.

Contents

Overture		vii
Chronology		xiii
1	The First Steps	1
2	The Dance Begins: *Breaktime*	15
3	The Flip Side: *Dance on My Grave*	31
4	A Canticle of Faith: *NIK: Now I Know*	49
5	A Ghostly Fugue: *The Toll Bridge*	67
6	Dance to the Music of Time: *Postcards from No Man's Land*	87
7	The Last Waltz: *This Is All: The Pillow Book of Cordelia Kenn*	105
Selected Bibliography		123
Index		127
About the Author		133

Overture

"I refuse to sell young people short by compromising on language or subject matter."[1] As Aidan Chambers indicated in this statement to the press about his "difficult" and "controversial" novel *Postcards from No Man's Land* when it won the 1999 Carnegie Medal, he respects his readers. He *trusts* them. At age fourteen or fifteen, he has said, "people can handle the same language as me, they're just as complicated as me, and are very interested in thinking about important questions for the first time."[2] He loves ideas, and language, and books that make you think; he knows that many, many young readers do, too.

When I met Aidan Chambers for the first time, as I was preparing to write this book, we sat in his modern, sparsely furnished living room—on one wall a shelf full of the books he loves, on another a beautiful wood carving of a quotation by one of his favorite writers, Samuel Beckett (a birthday present from his wife, I later learned), and outside, framed by a big picture window on the third wall, the stunningly beautiful Stroud valley in the Cotswolds of England, where he has lived for the last forty years. I felt that I already knew him, however, from reading his website, where he not only posts accounts of his recent travels and the books he has read but encourages others to chime in with their own recommendations. Books mean a lot to him. I already knew from his books that places do, too.

Seventeen-year-old Jacob Todd, an English boy whose story is half of *Postcards from No Man's Land*, falls in love with Amsterdam during the course of that book. The story that occupies the other half of the book takes place fifty-one years earlier when Geertrui, a nineteen-year-old Dutch girl, falls in love with Jacob's grandfather, an English soldier who has parachuted into the Netherlands during World War II. These two stories, which are told in alternating chapters and which touch on euthanasia, sexual identity, unmarried pregnancy, and other "difficult" issues, finally intertwine in unexpected ways. All different kinds of love, including love of place, are explored along the way. The telling, as it must be, is as complex as the stories. In neither language nor subject matter, as Chambers says, is there compromise.

"Difficult" is a word used often in writing about Chambers' novels. In just one review we find the words "intricate," "multi-layered," "provocative," "salty," "unreserved," "sophisticated," "mature"—in short, "difficult."[3] Chambers has long been recognized as a writer who doesn't make things easy for his readers but one who richly rewards the thoughtful reader who likes to be challenged. Reviews also use such phrases as "first-class reading," "elegantly written and full of ideas," "remarkably perceptive and compassionate," "brilliant and complex," "riveting and thought-provoking," "wide-ranging, challenging, beautifully written." His books have won the most important awards that books for young readers can win. Besides Britain's Carnegie Medal, the counterpart to the Newbery Medal given in the United States, Chambers has won the 2003 Michael L. Printz Award for best young adult novel (for *Postcards* when it was published in the United States) and, one year earlier, the Hans Christian Andersen Award, an international award given every other year in recognition of an author's body of work (sometimes called the counterpart in children's and young adult literature of the Nobel Prize). Chambers has made his mark in Britain, in America, and internationally. His books have been translated into fifteen languages.

These recent awards do not suggest, however, that Chambers is new on the scene or that his previous work has not been highly regarded. *Postcards* is the fifth in a series of six novels, begun in 1978 with *Breaktime*, continuing with *Dance on My Grave* (1982), *Now I Know* (1987; published in the United States as *NIK: Now I Know*), *The Toll Bridge* (1992), *Postcards from No Man's Land* (1999), and concluded with *This Is All: The Pillow Book of Cordelia Kenn* (2005). Chambers calls these six books his "Dance Sequence."

Each one of these novels in the series has been groundbreaking in its own way and has accordingly received a great deal of attention and critical acclaim. Perhaps his best-known novel before *Postcards* is *Dance on My Grave*, one of the first young adult novels to deal openly with a homosexual relationship between two adolescents. All of his novels, however, deal very openly with sexual themes. Chambers decided early on, he says, that literature "should be about all life, not only easily approved parts of it," so there would be "no taboos" in his writing. He says that he decided at the same time that there would be "no restrictions" in how a story is told—that is, each novel is in the form that story demands.[4]

Chambers calls these six novels the "Dance Sequence," but they are linked by ideas and themes, not by people and places. (Only in the last book does a character from an earlier book return.) Chambers says it is not essential that readers approach his books as a *sequence*, but that reading them in chronological order deepens the experience. He also says he thinks of the books as a family. The members are individuals with separate personalities but also genetically related to the other members. I have used his description in organizing this book—a chapter devoted to each distinct member, or book, and these chapters arranged according to the chronology of when the book was published. Because the books are thematically related, however, the chapters intertwine considerably. Chambers also uses another metaphor to explain how he sees these books as related. He says, "The image I usually use is that the six are like paintings in a gallery. One room, with six paintings on a wall. When you first see them, you think they are six separate pictures by the same artist. But after a while, and when you stand back for a final look before leaving, you realise that the six also make one big picture, the six being related in all sorts of ways and by all sorts of connections that you did not at first realise. And so you think again about them all."[5] Like a family. Like a room of paintings by the same artist. Whichever metaphor you choose, the books are related. Some of Chambers' themes and concerns that you will see repeated in all the books include:

> *Experimental structure and form*: The jury of the Hans Christian Andersen Award cited Chambers' "handling of varied narrative techniques." Chambers himself has admitted that how a story is told interests him as much as the story itself. Each of his novels is written in a different and unusual form, the form reinforcing the story.

Word play: Chambers has said there would be no concessions in language, and as a result his novels are full of linguistic twists and complexities. Often his protagonists are as fascinated with language as is Chambers himself, and so his readers are expected to be also. The sophistication of language in his books is a hallmark of Chambers' style and a measure of his respect for his readers.

Intellectually intense adolescents as protagonists: One focus of all the novels is on the interior life of the protagonist. The novels are about moral choices and finding a sense of self. They are about self-discovery—spiritual, philosophical, psychological, and sexual.

The complexity of gender and sexuality: This focus relates to the previous one, but because of Chambers' emphasis on it in all of his novels, it deserves special attention. All of the novels deal both with society's changing views of sexuality and the inward struggles of the characters with the complexities of sexual identity—with heterosexuality, homosexuality, and bisexuality.

Interpersonal relationships or friendship: All of Chambers' books have at their center personal relationships—or, in literary terms, character. Intriguingly, he has said that a traumatic moment in his life occurred when he was ten and was forced to move with his family away from the girl that had been everything to him— brother and sister, friend and lover.[6] His novels continue to explore the boundaries of identity and themes of separation and connection.

Indefinite conclusions: All of Chambers' novels are open-ended. Readers are left with questions and not answers, what one review calls "just a rich and painful confusion of what it means to be human."[7]

If Chambers' six novels for young adults are a dance sequence, then Chambers himself is a master choreographer. Just as a choreographer does, Chambers loves to find patterns in our experience. He sees patterns in movements, in language, in events. For example, in his acceptance speech for the Andersen Award he recounts all the coincidences he saw surrounding that event. When he speaks of how his books got started, his accounts are full of words like "happy accident." But he then turns around and imposes his own patterns on our experience. Like a choreographer, he makes his characters move in a certain way. The last book in his dance sequence, for example, is a *pillow book*, a kind of journal—lists, observations, reflections—kept by a character, based on the historical reality of books kept under their pillows by Japanese women in previous centuries who were not allowed to engage in any occupation. That structure organizes this part of the dance. Chambers finds patterns in our experiences and organizes his novels according to these patterns.

Aidan Chambers has choreographed a wide range of works, not just young adult novels. Along with the "Dance Sequence" of six novels written in the consciousnesses of young adults, he has also produced award-winning books for younger readers (*The Present Takers, Seal Secret*); plays that have been performed by young people of all ages; anthologies—especially of ghost stories; and nonfiction works for adults, which have achieved the same degree of critical acclaim as his novels. All of these works have in common a belief in challenging the reader with serious subjects investigated in a lively and complex style. Even his books for very young readers have moral questions and emotional relationships at their core. His anthologies of ghost stories suggest his fascination with the way the mind can be haunted. His plays take both approaches, sometimes exploring a dream logic similar to his ghost stories and sometimes taking a realistic look at how a character can come to a better understanding of self through story, as he shows in his fiction.

Chambers also has produced a large body of criticism for adults. These critical works are of a piece with his literary works, for in both he is a passionate advocate for young people. His articles, lectures, and essays have been collected in two companion volumes, *Reading Talk* and *Booktalk*, about which reviewers have written that they "enrich your understanding," "have remarkable things to say," and are to be enjoyed for their "range, eloquence and wisdom." He has also written very practical guides, underpinned by clearly explained theory, for teachers and librarians. These two books, *Tell Me: Children, Reading and Talk* and *The Reading Environment*, have joined his two other books of criticism as standard texts in many undergraduate and in-service courses for students, teachers, and librarians. In 1982 his dedication to literature and to young people was recognized when he and his wife Nancy won the Eleanor Farjeon Award for "Outstanding Services to Children's Books," in part for their journal *Signal* and the Thimble Press, internationally known and highly regarded sources of professional work on young adult literature.

In his criticism he argues passionately for adults to help young people discover the breadth and depth of the literary experience in order to expand their worlds and to help them make reading central to their growth. He also offers practical suggestions, in a critically sophisticated but accessible way, for how adults can do this. Chambers was one of the first writers to take young adult literary criticism seriously, as his books and his work with *Signal* and Thimble Press demonstrate. He has always argued for the necessity of offering thought-provoking, complex literature to young people, and his own fiction is just that. He refuses to sell young people short.

Aidan Chambers has sometimes been called the British Robert Cormier because of his complexity and mature themes. But that would be selling him short. He is a distinct individual, as each of his novels is. However, he is also related to the family of young adult literature, as each of his novels is related to the others. I hope that by considering all the forces that drive him—by looking at his life and his works—readers will come to a better understanding both of the writer and of his place in literature.

NOTES

1. "Aidan Chambers: Winner of the Carnegie Medal for a Book Published in 1999," *ACHUKA* (2000), 2. Retrieved from www.achuka.co.uk/special/chambers.htm on 14 February 2004.
2. "Aidan Chambers," *ACHUKA*, 3.
3. "Review of *The Toll Bridge*," *Publisher's Weekly* (19 June 1995), 62.
4. Aidan Chambers, personal website. Retrieved from www.aidanchambers.co.uk/jounalism/journalism1.htm. Originally published as "The Death of Populism," *The Bookseller* (14 July 2000).
5. Interview via e-mail correspondence with Betty Greenway, 20 June 2004.
6. Aidan Chambers, personal website. Retrieved from www.aidanchambers.co.uk/bio.htm.
7. Hazel Rochman, "Review of *Postcards from No Man's Land*," *Booklist* 98 (15 May 2002). Retrieved from http://archive.ala.org/booklist/v98/my2/57chambers.html on 14 February 2004.

Chronology

1934   Born December 27, in the country outside Chester-le-Street, a coal-mining town in the north of England, the only child of a woodworker (joiner) and a homemaker. Roams freely in the wood and fields by his home with bosom friend Marion—for ten years they were "brother and sister, friends and lovers."

1940   At age five starts school, but, unused to crowds, is "confused, anxious, unhappy, and afraid." "Hopeless" at arithmetic and reading.

1942   Moves to Church of England junior school where for a year he is regularly caned for failures in arithmetic.

1944   At age nine, words suddenly "come together" and he can read, the beginning of a lifelong love of books.

1945   Fails exam determining whether he goes to an academic "grammar school" or to a non-academic "secondary modern." Father becomes manager of a funeral service and moves with family to Darlington, an industrial market town twenty-five miles from Chester-le-Street. Feels betrayal at separation from Marion and life he knew. Spends holidays throughout teens walking the Yorkshire Dales (setting for *Breaktime*) and working on the farm of a distant relative.

1948   After doing well at Darlington's "secondary modern" school, transfers to Queen Elizabeth I Grammar School. Encounters life-changing teacher Jim Osborn, a passionate advocate for literature.

1949	At age fifteen reads D. H. Lawrence's novel *Sons and Lovers* and decides then and there to become a writer, beginning his first (later abandoned) novel.
1953	Graduates from school and serves mandatory two years national service in the Royal Navy.
1955	Begins teacher-training college in London, at Jim Osborn's suggestion, where he revels in the live theater. Writes *Everyman's Everybody*, his first play to be performed.
1957	Graduates and is appointed English teacher in charge of drama at a grammar school, Westcliff High School for Boys, in Southend-on-Sea (the setting for *Dance on My Grave*). Many of his young fellow teachers are practicing Christians.
1959	Is confirmed into the Anglican Church.
1960	Resigns job and joins twin brothers, Peter and Michael Ball, in founding the Community of the Glorious Ascension, a new-style monastery where members take ordinary jobs to work with young people, in Stroud, in the Cotswolds of England (setting for the monastic scenes in *Now I Know*).
1961	Becomes English teacher in charge of the library and drama at Archway Secondary Modern school in Stroud.
1963	Begins novel, *First Date*, intended for his teenage students, who need to "recognize themselves" in books.
1965	Writes and produces a play, *Johnny Salter*, in which his students act. Drama editor of Heinemann Educational Books sees a performance and publishes it the next year. Begins lecturing nationwide on literature and education and reviewing for magazines.
1966	Writes and produces another play, *The Car*, also published by Heinemann. Persuades Macmillan to publish novels under the series title Topliners, specially intended for "nonacademic" students like those he teaches. Commissioned to write *The Reluctant Reader*, a book about teens as readers.
1966–1982	General Editor of Topliners, Macmillan's series of fiction for reluctant readers.
1967	Ever more dedicated to his writing, resigns from the monastery. Meets Nancy Lockwood, his future wife, ed-

	itor of *Children's Book News*, a review magazine of books for children. Publishes *Cycle Smash*, a novel (Heinemann).
1968	Marries Nancy on March 30. Resigns his teaching post to become a full-time writer. Publishes *Marle*, a novel (Heinemann), and *The Chicken Run*, a play (Heinemann Educational Books).
1969	With Nancy begins magazine, *Signal: Approaches to Children's Books*, and Thimble Press. For the next fifteen years teaches night courses for teachers, writes articles and ghost stories, presents radio programs, and helps Nancy with publications for Thimble Press. Publishes *The Reluctant Reader* (Pergamon) and the edited anthology *Ghosts* (Macmillan).
1970–1982	Part-time lecturer, teaching evening courses for the Further Professional Studies Department, University of Bristol, England.
1971	Publishes *Haunted Houses*, stories (Pan) and the edited anthologies *World Zero Minus: An SF Anthology* (Macmillan), *Hi-ran-ho!: A Picture Book of Verse* (Longman), and *I Want to Get Out: Stories and Poems by Young Writers* (Macmillan).
1972–1984	Writes regular column for *Horn Book*.
1972	Publishes *Ghosts 2*, stories (Macmillan).
1973–1975	Radio writer and presenter of "Bookbox," a fortnightly program about children's books (Radio Bristol).
1973	Publishes *More Haunted Houses*, stories (Pan); *Introducing Books to Children*, nonfiction for adults (Heinemann Educational Books); and the edited anthologies *Ghosts and Hauntings* (Kestrel) and *In Time to Come: An SF Anthology* (Macmillan).
1974	Publishes *Great British Ghosts* and *Great Ghosts of the World*, stories (Pan).
1975	Moves into house in the village of Woodchester, where he and Nancy still live, and begins *Breaktime*, the novel that was to become the first book in the "Dance Sequence."
1976	Publishes the edited anthologies *Funny Folk: A Book of Comic Tales* (Heinemann), *Flyers and Flying* (Kestrel), and *Fighters in the Sky* (Macmillan). Radio writer and presenter of "Children and Books" (BBC Radio 3).

1977	Publishes *Ghost Carnival*, stories (Heinemann) and the edited anthologies *Cops and Robbers* (Kestrel) and *Men at War* (Macmillan).
1978	Receives the first Children's Literature Association (U.S.) award for outstanding literary criticism for the article "The Reader in the Book." Publishes *Breaktime* (Bodley Head) and the edited anthologies *Escapers* and *War at Sea* (Macmillan) and (under pseudonym Malcolm Blacklin) *Ghosts 4* (Macmillan).
1979	Publishes the edited anthology *Animal Fair* (Heinemann).
1980	Publishes *Seal Secret*, novel for young readers (Bodley Head) and the edited anthologies *Ghosts That Haunt You* and *Loving You Loving Me* (Macmillan). Television presenter of a program for schools, "Ghosts" (ITV). Television writer and presenter of "Long, Short and Tall Stories" (BBC-TV).
1981	Publishes *Plays, Considered as Literature as Well as Theatre, for Young People from 8-18 to Read and Perform*, nonfiction for adults (Thimble).
1982–1992	Visiting Lecturer, Westminster College, Oxford, England, where he establishes and teaches courses in children's literature.
1982	With wife Nancy is awarded the Eleanor Farjeon Award for services to children's books. Publishes *Dance on My Grave* (Bodley Head), second novel in the "Dance Sequence," the edited anthology *Ghost after Ghost* (Kestrel), and the play *The Dream Cage* (Heinemann Educational Books), performed by Bristol Old Vic Theatre School.
1983	Publishes *The Present Takers*, novel for young readers (Bodley Head).
1984	Publishes *Poetry for Children: A "Signal" Bookguide* (with Jill Bennett) (Thimble) and the edited anthologies *Shades of Dark* (P. Hardy) and *Out of Time: Stories of the Future* (Bodley Head).
1985	Awarded the Dutch Silver Pencil for *Seal Secret*. Publishes *Booktalk*, nonfiction for adults (Harper) and the edited anthology *A Sporting Chance: Stories of Winning and Losing* (Bodley Head).
1986	Awarded the Dutch Silver Pencil for *The Present Takers*.
1987	Publishes *Now I Know*, third novel in the "Dance Se-

	quence" (Bodley Head; in U.S. as *NIK: Now I Know*, Harper) and the edited anthologies *A Quiver of Ghosts* (Bodley Head) and *A Haunt of Ghosts* (also a contributor) (Harper).
1988	Publishes the edited anthology *Love All* (Bodley Head).
1989	With David Turton, an Australian children's bookseller, founds Turton & Chambers, a publishing firm specializing in translations of children's books.
1990	Publishes the edited anthology *On the Edge* (Macmillan).
1991	Publishes *The Reading Environment*, nonfiction for adults (Thimble).
1992	Publishes *The Toll Bridge*, fourth novel in the "Dance Sequence" (Bodley Head).
1993	Publishes *Tell Me: Children, Reading, and Talk*, nonfiction for adults (Thimble).
1994	Awarded Dutch Silver Pencil for *The Toll Bridge*.
1998	Publishes play *Only Once* (published by his own imprint, Line By Line), performed by students of Wycliffe College.
1999	Publishes *Postcards from No Man's Land*, fifth novel in the "Dance Sequence" (Bodley Head), which is awarded the Carnegie Medal. Awarded the Hans Snoek Prize for the Dutch-language stage adaptation of *The Toll Bridge*. Publishes his novel *The Present Takers* in *More Cool School Stories* (with Susan Gates and Marilyn Watts) (Red Fox).
2000	Awarded the Italian Andersen Prize for *Postcards from No Man's Land*, for best youth novel of the year.
2001	Publishes *Reading Talk*, nonfiction for adults (Thimble).
2002	Awarded the international Hans Christian Andersen Award given by IBBY for the body of his work. Awarded the Michael L. Printz Award for *Postcards from No Man's Land*, given for the best young adult novel published in the U.S. Publishes the edited anthology *Favorite Ghost Stories* (Kingfisher).
2003	Awarded doctorate, honoris causa, from University of Umea, Sweden.
2005	Publishes *This Is All: The Pillow Book of Cordelia Kenn*, the sixth and final novel in the "Dance Sequence" (Bodley Head).

Chapter 1

The First Steps

An e-mail came from Aidan Chambers just a couple of days before the turn of the new year 2005, wishing me a happy holiday and telling me some news: "I finished my book on Sunday, December 26 (at 4:45 P.M. precisely in fact!) and had my 70th birthday the next day. So two endings: and now for the beginning . . . ." The book he was referring to is *This Is All: The Pillow Book of Cordelia Kenn*, the last novel in what he has called the "Dance Sequence." The novel, as the title suggests, ends Chambers' series of six novels written in the consciousness of a teenager. His birthday ended a decade that has seen him awarded the most significant prizes an author for young people can be awarded. The fifth book in the Dance Sequence, *Postcards from No Man's Land*, won the Carnegie Medal, Britain's recognition of the most distinguished book for children or young adults, and also the Printz Award, given to the most distinguished book for young adults published in the United States. He has also received the Hans Christian Andersen Award, given to an author for the body of his or her work (sometimes called the "little Nobel").

Just when you would imagine that Chambers would be thinking about retiring, about hanging up his pen, he has instead been contemplating another series of novels, these written in the consciousness of "an old person," for as he says, "Old now is not like it used to be. It's a whole new and uncharted territory of human life. What could be more exciting than to map it in novels?"[1] Chambers likes challenges. And beginnings. He has to. His life has been filled with challenges, and with beginnings. Perhaps that's why he writes young adult novels, for he has said, "When you are in your teenage years you are consciously experiencing everything for the first time, so adolescent stories are all beginnings. There are never any endings."[2]

A HOPELESS STUDENT

Aidan Chambers was born in the north of England on December 27, 1934, the only child of working-class parents.[3] His father was a joiner, or skilled woodworker, his other male relatives miners, this being a coal-mining area. His mother and other female relatives were occupied with domestic duties. His house was not unlike the others in the village of Chester-le-Street, "two-up, two-down" he has called it, red brick in a row of twenty other red brick houses. His parents were not readers. They owned only five books: a Bible, a small dictionary, two handbooks on health and house repairs, and an illustrated *Aesop's Fables*.

As he was an only child and born at home, he was nervous in crowds (still is, he says). But he was completely comfortable with Marion, a neighbor only six months older. He grew up with Marion, the only other child nearby, roaming the woods that lined the steep valley across from their row of houses. It was a safe time, when all those who lived in the area were their "extended family" and when they could pop in and out of houses, grabbing sweets when they were hungry or watching the goings-on of the adults when they were bored with solitude. Chambers describes this time in his life as safe and circumscribed: "All of this was home, not just number five, all of this was ours—Marion's and mine—and we would gaze out from the prescribed boundaries like members of a nervous tribe beyond whose borders prowled other far more fearsome beings who were to be avoided at all costs" (*SAAAS*, 38).

He had reason to fear what lay outside of those safe boundaries. School was a "shock," he has said, a traumatic time for him. World War II began in September 1939, and early in January 1940, immediately after his fifth birthday, he started school, which became his own private war. He hated the crowded playtime. He didn't make friends. He hated even worse the lessons, which he just could not grasp. "Slow," his teachers called him. He couldn't seem to understand the point of learning letters of the alphabet and copying them onto a slate. He was "hopeless," he says, at arithmetic; in reading he could recognize individual words but couldn't put sentences together where they made sense to him.

He couldn't read a book fluently until he was nine years old. He vividly remembers the exact evening when he finally could. He had taken home a book from school as his teacher regularly demanded (they had always been returned unopened, for his teacher, "a sadist" who regularly beat him for failures in arithmetic, never asked anything about the book): Suddenly as he puzzled over the words on the page they became voices in his head telling a story. He credits this achievement not to his sadistic teacher but to an earlier teacher who used to read stories to her five-year-old students and then have them act them out. From this late beginning Aidan Chambers was to go on to become an avid, a voracious reader. Perhaps at first it seems ironic that a "slow learner" should become a great reader and a successful author, especially one of "challenging," "difficult" novels. Yet as an adult—a teacher, critic, and author—he has shown enormous sympathy for and understanding of "slow" students. As a teacher, he always read aloud to his students every day and used drama as a beginning to interpretation. He searched out books for teens when many weren't available, and he campaigned for publishers to make them available. And as an author, he has understood the value of story—of enjoyment—in challenging readers to explore what they might find difficult. He has never talked down to them.

There is one very specific way that his early experiences have colored his writing. Marion, he says, was everything to him; they were "brother and sister, friends and lovers."[4] Close friendship is a theme in all Chambers' work, most notably in *Dance on My Grave*, where Hal Robinson, the sixteen-year-old protagonist, thinks he has found in Barry Gorman the "bosom friend" that he has longed for all his solitary, only-child life, what Hal calls "an out-and-out, no-holds-barred, one-for-both and both-for-one, totally faithful, ever-present friend" (44). *The Toll Bridge*, too, has at its center a bosom friendship, as Chambers says it was called in his generation—a nonsexual very close friendship, though it has an erotic element, as he points out we see in Greek culture. Such friendship, Chambers says, "is one of the most intensely important human experiences . . . and it's very, very important to young people."[5]

Most of Chambers' protagonists are, like Hal, like Piers in *The Toll Bridge*, and like Chambers himself, only children, loners who look for, sometimes find, and often lose those "bosom friends." Chambers lost Marion when he was ten, when his father took a job as a funeral director in a town twenty-five miles away. He felt betrayed by the only people he had thought he could trust. "The day of the move,

13 May 1945, marks the end of my childhood. I have never since felt at home anywhere or completely trusted anyone" (*SAAAS*, 43).

THE ADOLESCENT

Because of his early education, which was generally very poor—his "sadistic" teacher being a good example—Chambers failed the important "eleven-plus" exam, which at that time determined whether British students were given an academic or nonacademic high school education. However, the teaching at the secondary modern high school in his new town was better, certainly kinder, than what he had experienced before, and the young Aidan did well, so well, in fact, that he was transferred when he was thirteen to the town's academic high school, the Queen Elizabeth I Grammar School. (British terminology is often different from American terminology; a British grammar school is an American high school.) And there the young Aidan experienced a new beginning. There he encountered the teacher who was to change his life.

Jim Osborn was a forceful, sometimes feared English teacher. Chambers describes him as "witty, sometimes cruelly so, unrelenting in his dedication to literature, and, to me, an inspiration" (*SAAAS*, 44). At his new school Chambers found himself surrounded by students who were highly motivated, some of whom were passionate readers, and impelled by the force of a charismatic teacher who took an interest in him. Jim Osborn pushed him into the Debating Society, where he lost his fear of public speaking, and into the Dramatic Society, thus introducing him to serious professional theater and to Shakespeare, where he developed his taste—already whetted by an early love of films—for performance. And Jim Osborn pushed him into buying a book every week to start his personal library, a habit Chambers still cherishes. (When I met him at his house, he would often mention a book that had had an influence on him and then point it out to me on his bookshelves. He is a lover, and *keeper*, of books.)

It was one of these books bought for his personal library when he was fifteen that made Chambers decide that he wanted to be an author. D. H. Lawrence's *Sons and Lovers* is a coming-of-age novel about the son of a miner and a woman determined that her son not go down in the mines, that he better himself by education and by reading. She encourages her son, Paul, in his artistic leanings; his father thinks she is making a sissy of him. Paul's bosom friend is a girl, Miriam, with whom he wanders over a countryside very near Chambers' own coal-mining area in the north of England. Everything in the book, Chambers says, was like his own life. He had never read anything like it before, and he was captivated. The next day he sat down and started his own novel. He never finished it, but the impulse never went away, even when he went to London to train to become a teacher, also at Jim Osborn's insistence. It's an interesting coincidence that Paul Morel, the hero of *Sons and Lovers*, also trains to be a teacher before abandoning the profession to be a writer, a path Chambers followed many years later.

Jim Osborn made such a powerful impression on Chambers that he named the English teacher in *Dance on My Grave* after him, and he gave him many of the qualities of Osborn: his scariness, his haughtiness, and above all his fastidiousness about the use of the English language. Osborn's influence went much farther than that, however. Osborn believed that someone who had read something—no matter what—must have an opinion, and he wanted to know what it was. He read aloud every day to his students, a practice Chambers had already learned the value of from his infant-school teacher and which he strongly advocated later when he came to write his first books on educational theory. And Osborn made his students examine every text in the minutest detail, Chambers recalls: "He demanded that language be used precisely, that all sentimentality be scorned, that we should not waste time reading books he regarded as other than first-rate" (*SAAAS*, 44).

To Chambers, Jim Osborn's influence was incalculable. From him he learned to be passionate about reading and to read widely. Chambers says of this teacher, "Jim Osborn believed that his job was to enable me to go where I could not go on my own as a reader and a writer, and to get there as quickly as possible. He expected my reach to exceed my grasp. He did not teach me what I already knew and give me more of what I already knew I liked. He helped me select what I read, trained my understanding of it, and revealed to me why he read what he read and how he read it."[6] Chambers also learned from Osborn to use the language carefully and fully, as his books show. In *Writers for Young Adults*, Ted Hipple calls his use of language "dazzling."[7] "At 15, people can handle the same language as me," Chambers has said, as he knows from his experience with

Osborn. To this day Chambers says that he has no hobbies because he doesn't need them—he reads, slowly, and he writes. Both are activities that don't end.

THE TEACHER AND WRITER

Jim Osborn had already decided that Chambers would train to be a teacher after high school, but first he had to serve his two years of compulsory national service, which he did in the Royal Navy, stationed in Portsmouth, England. Luckily, he didn't have much to do there, except read books from the second-hand bookshop across the street. Chambers remembers little else of the experience.

The next two years at a teacher-training college in London made more of an impact, especially all the glorious live theater just half an hour from where he lived. During this time he saw all the greats, both actors and plays, and tried his hand at producing and writing his own plays. His first publicly produced work was during this time, *Everyman's Everybody*, which Chambers now calls "a one-act piece of student pretension" (*SAAAS*, 45). And during it all he read.

Now comes yet another beginning. In 1957 Chambers finished the course and took a job teaching English and drama at Westcliff High School for Boys in Southend-on-Sea, a rather down-at-heels holiday resort for Londoners (and setting of *Dance on My Grave*). This was the end of adolescence and, Chambers says, "the beginning of an independent life which gave me the chance to become what I truly wanted to be: a skilled teacher and, above all, a published writer":

> As it turned out the following three years were the uncomplicatedly happiest of my life. I loved my work, enjoyed the town and being by the sea, did all the things I like doing. But what counted most was that for the first time, for the only time in my life, I found myself accepted by a group of friends, all of them young men just starting their careers, whose relations with each other were amusing, straightforward, sympathetic, generous, entirely without competitive rivalries, unfussily affectionate. All were critical readers, thinkers, talkers. And so exceptional as to be statistically unlikely, most of them were practicing Christians. (*SAAAS*, 46)

He was there for only three years, but he had a wonderful time. What convinced Chambers to leave Westcliff was the influence of his Christian friends. Chambers explains that he had always been interested in religion, but as a non-believer. He speculates that the Anglo-Catholic mass appealed to his sense of theater, and the King James Bible appealed to his love for great literature. His friends convinced him to investigate religion, almost as a scientific experiment. He describes his thinking in this way:

> How can one know anything as profound, as unavailable to easy answers as questions about God and belief and worship and religious "truth" unless one tries to live the dilemmas? If one never enters a church, how can one seriously claim to know anything about the experience of those who do? If one never prays, how can one discuss its efficacy? Religion, they argued, was, by definition, unknowable by intellectual means alone. One had to trust, had to live the experiment of faith in order to discover anything useful about God and the mystery of religion. (*SAAAS*, 46)

Chambers started going along to mass with a friend, in order to enjoy the theater and language, he says, but soon was "gripped." He asked to be confirmed in the spring of 1959.

What happened next Chambers can't explain except by recalling that he had always been a loner, had always enjoyed solitude, and had always believed that if you were going to do something you'd better do it completely and do it right. If you were going to really investigate Christian belief, you should enter it wholeheartedly. The simplicity of a monk's life and the absorbing quality of meditative prayer appealed to what Chambers now laughingly calls his "monastic personality." When he happened to hear of two brothers who were being trained as monks but who wanted a new-style community where the members held ordinary jobs working with young people, Chambers decided to resign his teaching job at Westcliff and join them.

THE MONK AND PUBLISHED AUTHOR

In August 1960 Chambers ended his teaching job in Southend-on-Sea and began his life as a monk in a large house in the middle of Stroud, in the Cotswolds of England, near where he has lived ever since. This period was to be, he says, "the hardest worked seven years" of his life. He was soon teaching English and drama full-time in the local secondary-modern school and simultaneously carrying on his monastic life at the Community of the Glorious Ascension. He was happy, but nagged from the start by a desire to get on with his teaching job at the expense of "the living heart" of monasticism, a *shared* domestic life whose core is daily worship in chapel.

Unknown to anyone except himself, when he joined the monastery he had decided to give up writing. He had not been successful, he reasoned—he would give up his ambition as his personal sacrifice to the monastery. For two years he wrote nothing, then he suffered something of a physical collapse. He at first thought it was the strain of his work, but the doctor who attended him dismissed the idea and guessed that there was something missing from his life. After a year he stopped taking the mild tranquillizers the doctor had prescribed and started writing *First Date*, a novel intended for his students. He had learned from his own experience of reading D. H. Lawrence's *Sons and Lovers* how powerful recognizing yourself in literature could be; he wanted to exploit this power with his own "reluctant readers," so the book was about kids like them—children of working-class families—with concerns like theirs: the rapidly changing social conditions of the early 1960s, including changing sexual mores.

There followed a play for his students to perform, *Johnny Salter*, which was a big hit. It was even seen by the drama editor of Heinemann Educational Books, who decided he wanted to publish it. Another play, *The Car*, followed, then another, *Chicken Run*. Chambers had finally persuaded Macmillan to publish a series of paperback novels intended for the kind of student that he taught, and that he himself had been, so in 1966 he became general editor of a series for reluctant readers. As he started to make a name for himself, he was more and more in demand as a speaker and as a reviewer for magazines. He was commissioned to write a book about teenagers as readers. All of these projects quite often took him away from Stroud and his monastic life there.

Something had to give, and Chambers knew it. His life as a teacher, lecturer, reviewer, editor—most of all, as a writer—couldn't coexist with the life of a monk. What was worse, he knew now that he wasn't a true believer. To spare the monastery further ordeal, on September 26, 1967, Chambers left letters for the brothers who had started the Community and walked out with even less than he had brought with him. He even left behind his treasured books that he had been collecting since he was fifteen. But he says that he never regretted his time as a monk and the perspective it gave him. In those short years, he has said, he learned more about himself and other people than at any time since.

Chambers has continued to have a great interest in the spiritual, as his novel *NIK: Now I Know* demonstrates. In that novel, the protagonist, Nik Frome, needs to learn more about himself, about faith, and about the girl he comes to care deeply about, a Christian who defines herself by her belief. Nik's journey of self-discovery involves a brief stay in a monastery modeled on the one Chambers joined. As the group of novels Chambers has come to think of as the "Dance Sequence" progressed into a comprehensive exploration of the different kinds of experience that lead to full consciousness and an understanding of the meaning of life, he knew that a novel based on the exploration of religion must be a part. He says a teenager's spiritual life is such an important though seldom talked about part of experience that "like sex, you can't leave it out."[8] Chambers continues to revisit the experience that occupied such a large part of his life in his last book in the sequence, *This Is All: The Pillow Book of Cordelia Kenn*, the only novel in which a character from a previous book returns. Julie, the girl Nik pursues in *Now I Know*, is a character in the sixth novel, a circumstance not planned, Chambers says: "It just happened. I suddenly realized who this person was—who I had thought was a different character. And suddenly I realized who she was. It's Julie from *NIK*—twenty years later."[9]

PARTNERS

Less than a month after Chambers quit the monastery he met his future wife. He had gone to London to see his publisher and decided to call in on Nancy Lockwood, editor of *Children's Book News*, as she had invited him to review for her magazine. They were like-minded in their equally passionate interest in books for young people. That day, he says, began a conversation that is still going on. They started corresponding daily; when he moved into his own apartment near Stroud (he had been living with friends after he left the monastery), he invited her to be a guest. They decided to get married soon after, at his parents' house on March 30, 1968.

With Nancy's encouragement Chambers gave up teaching to become a full-time writer. He had discovered early in his teaching career that it is not a job for a writer, because it is "exhausting" and takes the same energy as it does to write a novel. But they weren't quite sure what they wanted to do. They had taken a break from the world and gone to stay with Nancy's parents in New Hampshire. While collecting their energies they came upon Leonard Woolf's five-volume autobiography and were intrigued to find that he and his wife, the novelist Virginia Woolf, had started the Hogarth Press with practically no money. A press was what Chambers and his wife wanted to establish, and practically no money was what they had. They felt a need for a magazine that would try to raise the quality and broaden the range of critical writing about literature for children. But they'd always feared that they could never accumulate enough money to start it up and keep it going. After reading about the Woolfs, they said "Let's do it!" and so *Signal* magazine and the Thimble Press were born. With no publicity and no fanfare, the first issue was mailed out in January 1970 to a list of 500 people they thought would be interested.

ROOTS OF THE DANCE

For the next five years Chambers wrote articles, presented radio programs, edited Macmillan's series for teens, and taught night classes at Bristol University. Thimble Press developed a good reputation and became self-sustaining, allowing Nancy to even hire part-time workers to run it. However, there was another beginning Chambers didn't quite know how to engineer. He explains the crisis:

> My plan was to write another book of the kind I'd written before. But when I sat down to start I realized that the prospect so bored me I couldn't face it. What was worse, I knew my respect for myself was fading. What I was doing had ceased to be for those pupils I used to teach and had become hackery. I'd locked myself into the need to make money from something that meant too much to me to mistreat like that. For days I sat and worried while I looked out of the window at the green and sun-blazed valley. Finally, desperation took charge. Ordering myself about like an angry schoolteacher, I grabbed a brand-new notebook, a brand-new pencil (I usually typed everything I wrote), sat myself in an easy chair (I usually sat at a desk), and told myself to write the first thing that came into my head and to go on till I told myself to stop.[10]

The first words that came to him were the first words of *Breaktime*.

Chambers is the first to admit that he didn't have a clue about what he was doing. The book just "bubbled up." It was a long, slow process—over two years—until the book was finished. But it is, he says, "the book I regard as the first of my own" (*SAAAS*, 52). It was, as Chambers predicted, turned down by his regular publisher but immediately accepted by the Bodley Head, a publisher he had long admired for publishing James Joyce's *Ulysses*, Maurice Sendak's *Where the Wild Things Are* (it might scare the children, the other British publishers said), and other "risky" books. For *Breaktime* was risky, with its explicit sex scene and unusual narrative form. When it was published in 1978, however, its reception was extremely positive, without any of the anticipated criticisms materializing.

As is Chambers' habit, he had already started his next novel—he likes to know what he is doing next—but midway in writing *Dance on My Grave* he "intuited" that there would be a sequence of six books: "I began to see that these two novels were—seemed like—a pair. But then I saw that there were elements missing that would have been there if you could have written a great big book about the nature of adolescence. And that's when the intuition came that there would be six."[11] Each of these six has a long history, which I will explore in more detail in the following chapters, but their publication dates tell something of the length of time each took to complete. *Breaktime* was published in 1978, *Dance on My Grave* in 1982, *Now I Know* in 1987, *The Toll Bridge* in 1992, *Postcards from No Man's Land* in 1999, and, thirty years after the start of *Breaktime*, the sixth, *This Is All: The Pillow Book of Cordelia Kenn* in 2005. Each novel, he says, "is a different kind of love story—that's the principle of each one. There's a love story in each one, of a different kind."[12] And in each one, he goes on, "the world is looked at through the consciousness of a teenager, or a young adult. That's what makes them a youth novel [the term often used in Britain for the genre called "YA" in the United States]. It's not about audience; it's about the consciousness in the book."[13]

This group of six novels forms the core of Chambers' writing, but there have been many other books, "satellites" he calls them, along the way. Chambers explains that, because it takes him so long to prepare for and write a novel, he must have other projects so that he is not "suffocated" by a book (*SAAAS*, 54). During these years while he was completing the "Dance Sequence," he continued to be a very active speaker and essayist on issues in education, and many of these pieces are collected in *Booktalk* (1985) and *Reading Talk* (2001). He also wrote two practical guides for teachers and librarians, *The Reading Environment: How Adults Help Children Enjoy Reading* (1992) and *Tell Me: Children, Reading, and Talk* (1993), which have been used as classroom texts in many universities that train teachers. He is a highly regarded critic, shown by his award for "Outstanding Literary Criticism" given in 1979 by the International Children's Literature Association. A crucial aspect of Chambers' life is his work with students and teachers. He has never given up his teaching completely and has felt very lucky to have been asked to be a visiting lecturer in many schools and universities. For their work on behalf of literature for young people, he and his wife were given the Eleanor Farjeon Award in 1982, a very prestigious honor given for "Outstanding Services to Children's Books."

It wasn't until 1999, however, that his fiction began receiving the same kind of honors. In that year Britain's Carnegie Medal was given to *Postcards from No Man's Land*. When that book was published in the United States it won the Printz Award. In 2002 Chambers received the Hans Christian Andersen Award, given by the International Board on Books for Young People for the complete body of an author's work. In his acceptance speech for that award, he speculates on the connection between a writer's work and his or her life, taking Anne Frank, the favorite writer of the main character in *Postcards from No Man's Land*, as his example. It is no coincidence that Anne is also one of Chambers' favorite writers. Anne, he says, is "a brilliant storyteller." He continues:

> She does not need to invent weird fantasies to divert herself. She does not allow sentimentality to corrupt her view of life, quite the opposite. Anne is a great realist. She takes the world as she finds it—mouldy peas that have to be rubbed clean before they can be eaten, the loss of her treasured fountain pen, an argument with her parents. . . . She can take a few apparently boring everyday events such as these and show how fascinating they can be. She does this by the clarity of her thought, the precision of her use of language, and her inborn impulse as a teller of stories.

Anne, Chambers concludes, has written a record of "the human journey to self-consciousness. It is about every individual's discovery of self-knowledge."[14] When asked how he thinks his life has influenced his work, or how his work has reflected his life, Chambers says that he doesn't think his experience is very different from Anne's or from that of most writers:

> In a sense, I think that all writing is confessional, really. You disguise yourself. Some people are open about it; others pretend that their biography is just fiction. Poets I feel sorry for because their skin is totally open. That's why half of them are mad. [He laughs.] You see them on public platforms and think, poor man, he knows we're seeing into his soul. Well, I think fiction writers disguise. . . . But to me the whole business is about consciousness; it's about becoming more and more conscious, because I think that's the whole drive of the human race, that's what makes us different from the beasts, from animals.[15]

Writing is to help writers understand their life and to help readers understand theirs. To discover who they are and find their place in the world. To become *conscious*.

To that end, Chambers developed another rule for his writing, along with his rules of no concessions in language, no concessions in subject matter, and no restrictions on form. He says, "I won't write about a scene that I haven't myself direct experience of . . . by event or very, very close knowledge through observation of somebody else."[16] He puts himself in the tradition of realist writers who write about their own times. He dislikes fantasy and even historical fiction, refusing to write about what he has no knowledge of. He says, "Years ago, when I started *Breaktime*, I made a rule that whatever I wrote, whatever scene I 'invented', I would always have 'a reference point for truth' in my own life against which I can test the 'truth' of the scene I was writing."[17] He hopes that by the clarity of his thought, the precision of his use of language, and his inborn impulse as a teller of stories, he can make life fascinating and help us understand it better.

Chambers writes about characters who share his honesty, and his desire to understand themselves, life, and what it means to be human. That desire to understand was nourished by one special teacher fifty-five years ago, and now Chambers wants to do with his books what Jim Osborn did for him. Chambers has said, "Iris Murdoch, a philosopher and one of my favorite novelists, once wrote, 'Living is making distinctions and indicating order and pattern'. I would like my novels to help readers make distinctions in life, to indicate an order that enlivens them, and to find patterns that help them make sense of life."[18] That's what good choreographers do. They find patterns in the random, chaotic movements of life and make dances of these patterns. The rest of this text will explore those patterns in the "dances" of Chambers the choreographer—their characters, their forms, their language, their ideas. Let the dance begin.

NOTES

1. Aidan Chambers, personal website. Retrieved from www.aidanchambers.co.uk/faqs.htm.
2. Alison Brace, "Shock Tactics," *The Guardian* (London), 11 July 2000. Academic Search Premier. 14 February 2004. Keyword: Chambers, Aidan.
3. Most of the following information is taken from a personal interview with Aidan Chambers conducted by Betty Greenway on 14 December 2004 and from Chambers' autobiographical essay in *Something about the Author Autobiography Series*, vol. 12 (Detroit: Gale Research, 1986), 37–55, hereafter cited in the text as *SAAAS*.
4. Chambers, personal website. Retrieved from www.aidanchambers.co.uk/bio.htm.
5. Chambers, interview.
6. Chambers, personal website. Retrieved from www.aidanchambers.co.uk/journalism/journalism1.htm.
7. Ed. Ted Hipple, vol. 1 (New York: Scribner's, 1997), 219.
8. Chambers, interview.
9. Chambers, interview.
10. Chambers, interview.
11. Chambers, interview.
12. Chambers, interview.
13. Chambers, interview.
14. Andersen Award acceptance speech, reprinted on www.aidanchambers.co.uk/journalism/journalism3.htm.
15. Chambers, interview.
16. Chambers, interview.
17. Chambers, personal website. Retrieved from www.aidanchambers.co.uk/faqs.htm.
18. Chambers, personal website. Retrieved from www.aidanchambers.co.uk.faqs.htm.

Chapter 2

The Dance Begins: *Breaktime*

The beginning of *Breaktime* was an outpouring. It erupted. As the story in the first chapter of this book describes, Chambers was not happy with what he had been writing, so in desperation he *made* himself sit down, with writing tools and in a location purposely violating all he had been used to when he wrote, and put down the first thing that came into his head: " 'Literature is crap,' said Morgan." He didn't know who Morgan was. He didn't know what Morgan was talking about. A few pages later, Chambers had a scene involving two boys, one of whom seemed to be the protagonist but for whom Chambers had no name so he called him "Ditto." This "psychic shock," as Chambers calls it, became what we know as the first scene in *Breaktime* (*SAAAS*, 51–52).

As Chambers explains the process of starting to write *Breaktime*, "It was fairly unconscious. I didn't quite understand what was happening at the time."[1] Chambers needed to understand, so about a third of the way through the book, he stopped. He had to find out what he thought he was doing. The book did not continue to pour out. In fact, the conception may have been swift, but the birth was long and difficult. "It took me ages," he says, "another six months to try and work out what I was doing. Then I did the second third *thinking* I knew what I was doing, so I had to stop *again* because I didn't. Then I got the last third in and did the rewrite because it was clear to me what I was doing."[2] As this story demonstrates, Chambers is a very conscious artist. He thinks through what he is writing. The book may be one where the emotions of the main character are very much on the surface, but the author of that book has carefully shaped it.

Morgan's challenge to Ditto that "literature is crap" goads Ditto into an attempt to prove him wrong. Morgan argues that fiction, which is what he means by "literature," is just a game played by those who want to avoid life, and thus truth. As Margery Fisher notes in an early review of *Breaktime*, Morgan thinks that fiction "misses truth by its conventions, its tidy rendering of the untidy fabric of life."[3] Morgan's challenge coincides with two other difficulties in Ditto's life: his relationship with his seriously ill father is a very troubled one about which Ditto feels responsible to a degree and so he feels terrible guilt, and at seventeen Ditto feels his virginity as a burden to be rid of as quickly as possible. The last of these burdens Ditto has a chance to shed if he accepts the invitation of a girl he knew in school but who has since moved away. If he accepts the invitation, he can also escape from his father for a while, or so he hopes. And if he writes down his experiences while on the short trip meant to accomplish the loss of his virginity, he might be able to demonstrate to Morgan the value of literature as a vehicle to truth.

An exploration of how these three strands come together reveals something about Chambers as a shaper, about what he needed to learn and what he learned in order to shape—or choreograph, to continue with the metaphor—his novel into the first movement of the "Dance Sequence."

USE OF AUTOBIOGRAPHICAL ELEMENTS

Breaktime is Chambers' most autobiographical novel. The description of Ditto's room and of his house, the "three-bedroom, semi-detached, late 1930s, speculation-built house, half limey brick, half crumbling pebble-dash with bay-window on ground floor,"[4] is an accurate picture of the one Chambers lived in during his teenage years when his father moved the family to Darlington. The Yorkshire Dales around Richmond where Ditto goes camping and meets up with Helen, the girl with whom he plans to lose his virginity, is an area Chambers knows intimately from his teenage summers spent working on his cousin's farm and roaming the countryside. Ditto's and Morgan's literature teacher, Midgely, is a portrait of Chambers' profoundly influential teacher, Jim Osborn, in the way he rivets Ditto's attention, the way he is ruthless in marking essays, and the way he never makes concessions (8). And Midgely makes the same arguments that Jim Osborn did to Chambers' schoolmates: "[L]iterature offers us images to think with . . . , its unreality has nothing to do with untruth" (4). Morgan thinks Midgely is a "pompous ass," and he disagrees.

Chambers' own literary heroes are also Ditto's. For example, Jane Austen is the author Ditto has been reading when his father needles him about being "too thick" to understand. In *Introducing Books to Children* (1973), Chambers explains why Austen was so important to him in his formative years as a reader: "Here was a world and a collection of people so strange that I was spellbound with fascination, as an explorer might stand staring at a new land and an alien race. And the further I went into that foreign domain the more I began to recognize facets of behaviour, motivations, characters, which struck familiar chords. Jane Austen taught me the power of literature to open up different worlds, strange people, while at the same time showing the relationship of those worlds and people to the world and people I know and belong to."

Austen is Chambers' example of the subversive power of literature: that it challenges our prejudices and ingrained attitudes.[5] One of those ingrained attitudes Chambers argues against in *Introducing Books to Children*, published just two years before *Breaktime*, is the attitude we see Morgan and Ditto's father holding: that words and reading are somehow a substitute for action "more akin to the experience of a peeping Tom, an impotent voyeur watching healthy, active people get on with real living" (*Introducing*, 11). As Ditto's father shouts during the argument that brings on his heart attack, Ditto is a "twit" because he knows nothing except from books. Ditto recalls his father's words exactly: "Clever, I might be, but, using a favorite phrase of disparagement, if I were faced with a real life problem, I wouldn't know whether to have a shit or a haircut" (26).

Chambers' example in that earlier book of criticism for adults of the other essential value of literature—the conciliatory value of literature, "comforting us in our shared humanity"—is D. H. Lawrence's *Sons and Lovers*, a work we have already seen to be *the* most important work in Chambers' desire to be a writer. Chambers calls it "an elutriate," "clarifying myself to myself as well as showing me I was not alone" (*Introducing*, 10). In *Breaktime* Ditto sees on his bookshelf Orwell, Lawrence, Joyce, and Richard Brautigan, all authors who, it is interesting to note, write autobiographical works early in their careers, as Chambers is doing, and, in the case of Lawrence and Joyce, these early works are *bildungsromans* tracing the journey each protagonist makes to become an artist, in both cases journeys in conflict with their fathers. Ditto, however, sees these books now as accusers, in a way, artifacts of boyhood crazes and passions, like the old pictures on his wall, and "bought more—could it really be the truth?—because he believed they were what he should read and possess rather than simply to please himself" (22). The journey Ditto makes to the Yorkshire Dales to lose his virginity is truly a journey of maturation, where he casts aside, as Lawrence comes to do in his later novel *Women in Love*, even those ideas of his youth that make him want to mature in the first place. As Chambers admits of this first novel he sees as truly his own, with his own voice, *Breaktime* has "all the influences in it I had when I was sixteen."[6]

CHARACTER AS DOUBLENESS

Like literary influences and settings, Chambers' portrayal of Ditto's character is also highly autobiographical. In the section of the book called "Who Is Ditto," the physical description is very much like Chambers at the same age. Ditto is "thin, wiry, given to being lanky." He is brown-haired and green-eyed, pale, with a slim nose and wide mouth. More significant, their personalities are remarkably similar, down to hating dentists and being self-conscious about the glasses needed for short-sightedness, thin legs, and jutting chin. And like all of the main characters in Chambers' novels to come, Ditto is something of a loner, feeling no need to belong to what he calls "mobs of people" (36–38). He is also highly articulate, as are his friends. His conversations with Morgan that bookend the novel as well as those with the two boys he meets on his journey, Newcastle Jack and Robby, may even sound a little too precocious and unreal, as several critics have complained (Geraldine DeLuca calls them "overbearingly self-conscious"[7]). As other critics have pointed out, however, these conversations are no different from those held by Stephen Dedalus and his friends in *A Portrait of the Artist as a Young Man* by James Joyce (Richard Yates calls them "pretentious" but accurate to the way many young intellectuals talk[8]). Joyce is another of the authors Ditto has on his bookshelf and an important influence both on Chambers and on this novel, as we will see when we come to talk about its style. Chambers confirms the autobiographical nature of these conversations when he recounts the endless talks on philosophical ideas that he and his friends had in school, in teacher-training college, and in his first teaching job.[9]

Not only are the young characters smart and articulate, they are also aware, tuned into their own inner beings, which they often feel to be divided. Helen says to Ditto, "It's as though two people are inside me, quite different people who have to take it in turns at being me. . . . [O]ne of them is always wanting to go new places, meet new people, do new things. The other is scared of all that, is shy, I suppose, afraid, never sure of herself, not wanting to fail and always feeling she has" (155–56). When Ditto says flippantly, "Can't I have both?" Helen replies seriously, "I've never tried being both at once before. Is it possible, do you think?" (156). That question runs throughout Chambers' books, which are filled with doubles, Dr. Jekylls and Mr. Hydes, secret sharers.

Joseph Conrad's short story "The Secret Sharer" is particularly relevant to one of the story strands in *Breaktime*, the encounter with Jack and Robby. In Conrad's story, the new captain of a ship on watch late at night, alone, sees a naked swimmer approaching. When he takes the man on board and shelters him, we learn that the swimmer is a wanted man, for he has killed the captain of his own ship for endangering his men. Our captain, sympathetic to this man's plight, contrives to hide him from the rest of the crew so that he is never seen. As more of the man's story comes out, the two discover that they share a similar background—the same town, the same school, and so on. The captain determines to try to save the man by steering dangerously close to an island so that he has a fighting chance of swimming to it in safety. As the fugitive swims away in the captain's clothes, his hat caught in the current allows the captain to see where to safely steer. The short story is generally seen as allegorical—the "secret sharer," or other side of the captain's personality, makes it possible for this young, raw captain, who has been continually questioned by his men, to take "command" for the first time and come into his own.

The boy Ditto meets on his journey, Robby, is, like the secret sharer, a "bad seed," yet, with that "underskin of violent energy, that blush of fanatic charm," strangely attractive, tempting Ditto into drinking more than he is able, disrupting a political gathering, and finally, completely against all reason, robbing the guest speaker's very elegant house, which, Robby argues, is living proof of the hypocrisy of the speaker's professed Marxist beliefs. Robby even talks Ditto into stealing a rare and expensive edition of Marx's *Das Kapital*, a fitting symbolic gesture, as his friend notes. Ditto shares with Robby a very difficult relationship with his father, who, it turns out, was the keynote speaker at the political rally and the man whose house they rob. When they are caught by the father, Ditto thinks because of a "Freudian slip" when Robby drops a vase, the similarities between the two become apparent. Ditto watches Robby with his father and thinks:

> Robby was still unmoving, his face an agony of anger frustrated by filial embarrassment. I recognized that look at once, I had felt it so often myself. But was this really how one appeared at such times? So peevishly crushed, so lacking in control? So ugly? Just as I recognized the look on Robby's face, the whole gripped-in stance of his tense body, so I knew too that inside he was a seething confusion of feelings and thought: resentment and self-pity and a desperate but ineffective desire to hurt, yet, at the calm centre of his being, also wishing that none of this were so. Regretful that his father and himself had come to such a pass. . . .
> In that second Robby had shown me myself. (120–21)

As if "looking in a mirror," Ditto sees Robby and suddenly understands his own situation. (Mirrors become increasingly important in Chambers' next novel, *Dance on My Grave*, as an image of doubleness.) Immediately after that, Ditto has his first sexual experience and then resolves to go back home to his father, with whom he is able to empathize for the first time. In his room he puts away everything that represents his past. The implication is that Ditto's recognition, the end point of his journey, allows him to "come of age," in the same way that the captain in "The Secret Sharer" comes of age as a result of his encounter with his double. As a reviewer says, "Ditto on coming home is a stronger and more compassionate boy than when he left."[10]

DIFFERENT KINDS OF LOVE

As in all of Chambers' novels, the protagonist faces another kind of doubleness—what can be called a confusion of sexual identity. Ditto has taken this journey to lose his virginity with a girl he once knew and admired, but he is drawn to the two boys he meets on the way, boys who hint at their homosexuality. When Ditto is offered something to eat, for example, he replies, "Not for me, thanks, . . . I had something in the castle," his new friend laughs, "Not our Jack, I hope" (65). Ditto notices details that imply his attraction: the first boy's tanned, muscled body and his shirt "open to the fourth button," the second boy's handsome face. And he is curious about homosexual sex, as he shows when he asks himself in a half-drunken stream-of-consciousness monologue: "Don't know what to make of them two, those two, are they? Dunno. Interesting. What do they do? if?" (70). But in this book by Chambers, unlike those to come, the complexity of gender is not pursued; it is just one more complexity in the complex mix of personality. It's part of what Ditto is asking when early in the novel he says, "WHO was the present Ditto?" (22). And it's what he concludes at the end: "Everybody's being is like a collage" (147). It's part of the ongoing search for identity that is at the heart of all Chambers' novels.

An important aspect of that search for identity is, as Chambers has remarked about all of the novels in the "Dance Sequence," an exploration of the nature of love. In this novel, heterosexual love is dominant, as the end scene with Ditto making love to Helen suggests, but the nature of the love between father and son is also an issue. Relations between Ditto and his father have definitely soured, to the point where neither can remain calm during a conversation. Both are unhappy about that: "It pains Ditto; he is certain it pains his father. But the hurt is apparently incorrigible" (10). In between the regular shouting matches, as is Ditto's habit, he recounts memories that pop into his head.

For example, on his way home from school on his bike, Ditto is "pedaling steadily towards his next parental encounter," but his thoughts "travel in another direction" (10). He remembers a photograph of a fishing trip when he was ten, and the photograph triggers memories of the trip itself. His father is proud of Ditto for catching his first fish, a dace, and asks a nearby angler to take a picture so that he can be in it, too. But just after the picture is taken, Ditto and another boy see and kill a grass snake by savagely throwing stones at it, against his father's quiet advice that the snake is harmless. This time his father refuses to get in the photograph that Ditto wants taken. Ditto says, "If not the snake why the dace?" (12). He is morally confused, but he feels his father's stern disapproval, which is communicated by silence.

Back in the present, when Ditto reaches home we are given an example of the tensions between them, in Ditto's sad recognition that his father really doesn't know who Jane Austen is and his father's prickly accusation that his son thinks he is "too thick" to understand. His father, coughing in an armchair in a room smelling of "rancid snot, stockinged feet, and overheated television set," is reduced, when accepting Ditto's offer of a cup of tea, to a "small boy ashamed" (14). The pattern is one Chambers says he got from the characteristic Shakespearean comic plot: "Young people in rebellion against waning adult authority. . . ."[11] At the end of the book, after Ditto's journey, he turns his feet toward home, "[T]he only one I have. For now" (168). As Chambers goes on to say about this Shakespearean plot, the young people return, "changed and closer to achieving their personal independence, to the regulation and order of the adults from whom they will shortly take over the running of society."[12] Tension is inevitable, this story of fathers and sons tells us, "growing pains" as Ditto's father perceptively calls it in his loving letter to Ditto at the end: "You are growing up and I am growing old" (172). Ditto feels a "grieving love" for his father, but the grief is both for the father and for the son.

The novel also questions the whole nature of love when it raises the question of altruism. Ditto is upset because he feels that Robby has simply used him in his fight with his father. But Robby's friend counters that Ditto must have been using them, too. Ditto silently agrees as he thinks of the reason he goes along with Robby in the first place: "*Experience. It's all experience*" (124). He later tells Helen what Robby's friend said, that "we are all users, that everybody uses everybody else . . . that there's no such thing as altruism," and he asks her whether she believes that (158). Since Ditto asks Helen this in the moments of their sexual foreplay, there is the distinct suggestion that they are using each other. If sex isn't altruistic, perhaps love isn't either.

HOW THE STORY IS TOLD

As Chambers' reference to Shakespeare makes clear, *Breaktime* is much more than an autobiographical outpouring. It has been carefully shaped. "I wanted to avoid the snare always waiting for novelists," Chambers says in his essay "From Writer to Reader: An Author Reads Himself," "the temptation to evade problems of invention by disguising autobiography as fiction."[13] In that essay Chambers discusses the structures of *Breaktime* and *Dance on My Grave*. Writing those novels, he says, "taught me how to use autobiography in the creation of a fiction without turning the fiction into autobiography. In other words, it taught me how to use myself to write truth in fiction while also keeping my distance."[14]

The two authors who most inform *Breaktime*—they are on Ditto's bookshelf and are referred to in the book, either directly or indirectly—are James Joyce and D. H. Lawrence. And as we've seen, they have both written highly autobiographical novels. To take just one example—setting—Lawrence thinly disguises his own town of Eastwood in Nottinghamshire as Bestwood in *Sons and Lovers*, whereas Joyce's *Ulysses* so accurately reproduces the Dublin of his time that, as he says, if it were completely wiped off the map you could perfectly reconstruct it from his novel. Chambers, too, says that you could go around any of his settings with book in hand as a guide. However, Joyce and Lawrence are, as Chambers is, more interested in ideas than events, in philosophical significance, and they are more interested in language, how something is communicated, than in plot, what happens. Chambers explains how this interest manifests itself in *Breaktime*: "*Breaktime* is not so much about event or character as it is about states of being: the state of being adolescent, the state of being a son and a would-be lover, the state of being drunk and of being an amateur burglar, of being a seducer and of being seduced, and so on. Just as Shakespeare's comic plot controls the overall narrative pattern, so the examination of each episode as a state of being controls the narrator's focus of attention. This determines what he chooses to tell about, and how he tells about it."[15] Chambers' greatest interest, as he suggests here, is in consciousness, in who tells the story, how, and why.

Thus, the central question in *Breaktime* becomes what is fact and what is fiction, as Morgan's challenge spells out: "Literature is, by definition, a lie. Literature is a fiction. Fiction is opposite to fact. Fact is truth" (6). Therefore, literature is crap. The journal that Ditto keeps on his journey is meant to refute that charge. It will record events in any style that seems suitable, not in the literal, "logical" way Morgan ridicules, and it will demonstrate that fiction can seriously reflect the truth. Ditto's journal is in essence *Breaktime*. And true to his word, it uses many, many ways of telling.

"How a story is told," Chambers writes, "is as important as what it tells."[16] *Breaktime*, as a number of critics have noted, is told like an adolescent *Ulysses*, a fact Chambers calls attention to in a footnote written by Ditto himself. There Ditto admits that he got the idea for the way his journal is structured from Flann O'Brien, who got it from James Joyce ("I've discovered that almost all the interesting things contemporary writers do they get from his *Ulysses*"), who probably got it from Duns Scotus "or one of those forgotten Jesuit theologians Joyce was brought up knowing about." As Ditto says, "there is nothing new in this world" (54). A brief summary of *Ulysses* demonstrates the parallels between it and *Breaktime*. In *Ulysses* Joyce moves the Greek story of *The Odyssey* to Dublin, and he makes his hero a twentieth-century Jewish businessman, Leopold Bloom, who, in one day instead of ten years, is traveling home to his waiting Penelope, Molly. Each chapter, named after an episode in *The Odyssey* (Aeolus, Cyclops, Sirens, etc.), employs a different literary style (for example, the Aeolus chapter, set in a newspaper office, is written in all headlines). There are plays on words, flashbacks and flashforwards, jokes, parodies, chapters that are written in all clichés, or chapters in which there is all dialogue, followed by all interior monologue, then Socratic questions and answers, and so on. Along the way, not so incidentally, there is a stream-of-consciousness masturbation scene when Leopold watches a girl on the beach, similar to Ditto's scene when he looks at Helen's picture.

Chambers uses many of these same linguistic techniques, but of course as a young boy would write *Ulysses*. Chambers defends himself against the charge of "self-consciousness" in the writing—that the novel relies on mechanical tricks and is contrived—by reminding us that teenagers are often self-conscious when they write: "They imitate their favorite authors and are sometimes pompous; they over-decorate and look for unusual words and modes of expression. . . . This kind of self-consciousness is so typical of a boy like Ditto that no writing that is supposed to be his can avoid it. Finding this style, finding *his* voice, was important to me."[17] As even a quick glance at the book will reveal, there are many visual "oddities": the type changes; there are drawings, footnotes, and handwriting; columns of type bisect the page, with unvoiced thoughts set against text from a book or an interior monologue set against a conversation; there are stream-of-consciousness passages where the words are run together. The graphematic elements that call attention to the physical object as a book are quite various. Within these elements readers find blurbs from travel brochures, an excerpt from a Dr. Spock sex manual, and a passage from the burglary scene in *Oliver Twist*, as well as many other quotations and allusions. Ditto's formal "Reply to Morgan's Charges" explains why his journal won't be written "in the manner of our logical stories," for he says, "It shall take what form it cares for at any moment—which means whatever form I feel like giving it at the time of writing. . . . I shall use whatever styles of prose—or verse, or writing of any kind—I wish to use and which seems best for what I want to say"(35).

In this way Chambers makes his own interest in form and structure belong to his protagonist. In an article discussing an important trend in recent American young adult literature, where a number of award-winning novels depart from accepted narrative convention, Lauren Adams singles out the early works of Aidan Chambers, among them the 1978 *Breaktime*, as "groundbreaking." She writes, "Chambers gives tremendous attention to how the story is told, but only as the story itself prescribes. Chambers' interest in narrative technique is passed directly to his protagonists; the author's ambition to reflect life in literature as truthfully as possible becomes a challenge for his characters, an inextricable part of their own stories."[18] Adams reminds readers of the many recent young adult novels that employ variations in form, from novels written as poems—both structured and free-verse—or plays; to those with second-person narrators—both reliable and not; to those that defy brief description: Walter Dean Myers' *Monster*, Chris Lynch's *Freewill*, Virginia Euwer Woolf's *Make Lemonade* and *True Believer*, An Na's *A Step From Heaven*, A. M. Jenkins' *Damage*, David Klass' *You Don't Know Me*, Paul Fleischman's *Seek*, and others. Chambers was certainly in the forefront of these innovations, but, as he reminds readers in the footnote in *Breaktime*, none of this is new to literature—"there is nothing new in this world"—only to the relatively conservative genre of young adult literature at the time he was writing these early books.

The reference to Joyce's *Ulysses*, which uses many of these same techniques, and to Flann O'Brien, which Ditto reads with "puzzled pleasure," hints at the attitude the author hopes readers will take to *Breaktime*. Anyone who likes puzzles will enjoy "puzzling out" the many meanings of names, for example. The fragmented format of the book is suggestive of one of the several meanings of "breaktime," for the narrative breaks strict chronology. Ditto also travels on a break from school, the half-term holiday. He sits with Morgan at the end, watching "the breaktime mayhem in the playground below" (178). And the novel recounts the time when Ditto breaks from his parents, as he shows when he thinks of his father's heart attack: ". . . whatever the cause of the trouble, a break would have happened between them sometime anyway. After all, he had to gain his independence somehow" (83). Chambers himself comments on the characters' names in his essay "From Writer to Reader: An Author Reads Himself," a fascinating study of ways an author tries to enrich the reading of a work, in the same way, Chambers says, that a walker over interesting countryside can enjoy the immediately visible sights or choose to investigate the geological foundations that lie hidden beneath the ground. The name "Helen" calls up Helen of Troy, the temptress who appears before Ditto dressed as a "desirable cliché" (143), after sending photographs and letters, first taking possession of him and then abandoning him. The man who ejects the drunken Ditto from the political rally is called by Robby "our Hector," the leader of the Trojans in the war that is begun because of Helen. Robby is, of course, the robber, and we discover that his last name is Hode, the old spelling of Hood. This Robin Hood also wants to take from the rich—his father—"take some of his unequal wealth and redistribute it" (108).

Ditto's name points to the fact that this is a book about language more than anything else. The word "ditto" means a repetition symbolized by marks ("), or a little picture drawn on a page. Thus, the person Ditto is just a drawing, or marks on a page. In his essay Chambers calls readers' attention to a passage in *Through the Looking-Glass*, that most linguistic of books, where Alice talks to Tweedledum and Tweedledee about the sleeping king before them. Tweedledee says that the king is dreaming about Alice; if the king were to wake she would "go out—bang!—just like a candle" because she is only a thing in his dream. When Alice asks indignantly "if *I'm* only a sort of thing in his dream, what are *you* . . . ," Tweedledum says "Ditto," and Tweedledee says "Ditto, ditto" (qtd. in *Breaktime*,103).[19] When Morgan asks after reading about himself in Ditto's journal at the end of *Breaktime*, "Are you saying I'm just a character in a story?" Ditto replies laughing, "Aren't we all?" Readers are left with a question, not a dogmatic answer, as in all of Chambers' novels, but a very philosophical question about the nature of reality and language.

Chambers also hopes that readers will have the same response to "difficult" language, puns, and literary allusion as he does. *Break-*

time, for example, uses such words as "rodomontade," "concupiscence," "elutriating," "anti-dithyrambic," and "coloratura." Morgan, Ditto thinks, has had sex, "with his willy or nilly" (21). The chapter break immediately following Ditto's masturbation is "Afterbath" (21). Ditto calls his admission that he both loves and hates his father and that he fears sexual intercourse a "laundry list of emotional dirty linen," symbols of his "rag-bag being" (33). The weather is "suntillating" (56). Robby calls his friend "Jack the dripper" after he swallows his pint of beer at one go (64). Jack's father "brings him up by hand," the joke Dickens makes about the physical abuse Pip suffers in *Great Expectations* (65). A long passage from the burglary scene in *Oliver Twist* is inserted into the text, as Ditto apparently drifts off into his own thoughts while Robby is explaining the burglary they are going to do (114–15). In berating himself for making Helen run away the first time—for he realizes that he always says things to prevent people coming too close—Ditto echoes what Polonius says about the mad Hamlet: "True. It is. Pity 'tis. Twit" (79). The last section is called "END GAME," when written as one word the title of a Samual Beckett play. These and many, many other linguistic acrobatics are a feature of *Breaktime*.

They are there because Chambers, as he has said, refuses to condescend to his readers. "I'm a disciple of Shakespeare," he says, "and I'm still looking up references that I don't get. Of course you do that with any book that matters. You're going to have to do that. You can't read James Joyce without doing that, for instance. . . . If you really want to read him, you do that. And I said to myself, any kid who is capable of reading, from the age of fifteen on, is capable of doing anything with the language that I can do, or anything I ask them to do. So I won't make a compromise. I'll do what the book requires. And each book has a different language. It has its own linguistic manner."[20]

END GAME

Has Ditto successfully refuted the charge that fiction has nothing to do with truth? Has Chambers successfully re-shaped his own youth to provide readers with a convincing demonstration that literature can and should hold a central place—Chambers would say *the* central place—in our ongoing attempt to make sense of life? Chambers has provided one compelling answer to those questions in an essay he wrote before he began *Breaktime*, "Introducing Books to Children: Why Bother?": "When we come to deal with our imaginings, our thoughts, emotions, past experiences in an attempt to sort them out . . . , until we have forged these experiences into words we are not sure what we think, feel, know. . . . Without language . . . no one would have a chance; we would go bumping round in the dark, and eventually take leave of our senses under the welter of the incomprehensible, withdrawing, as some people do, into a closed world in order to protect ourselves against the unbearable onslaught" (*Introducing*, 177). Ditto answers by, in essence, calling Morgan's bluff. Fact can't be superior to fiction, as Morgan says at the beginning, because he can't tell the difference between the language of fact and the language of fiction in the end, after reading Ditto's story. He doesn't know what's "real" and what's not. Literature is just as real as life.

Chambers is doing something very Shakespearean here. Woven throughout Shakespeare's plays, his comedies especially, is a preoccupation with questions of reality and illusion. Sometimes a comparison is made between life and play-acting, as in "All the world's a stage, and all the men and women merely players" from *As You Like It*. Often life is compared to a dream, as in "We are such stuff as dreams are made on" from *The Tempest* or "Thou hast nor youth nor age, but, as it were, an after-dinner's sleep, dreaming on both. . . . What's yet in this that bears the name of life?" from *Measure for Measure*. All of *A Midsummer Night's Dream* plays with the idea that things that seem real may be as insubstantial as dreams. Chambers' novel is concerned with the same philosophical questions.

Ditto begins his journey, as we begin ours, unable to sort out "thoughts, emotions, past experiences." When he returns with what Morgan calls his "masterwork," his writings, whether he has taken a physical journey or not, in recreating the texture of his mind—what Chambers would call his consciousness—in making a story out of it, Ditto has captured, for himself and for readers, what it is like to be Ditto. He is now a little more aware of his thoughts, emotions, and past experiences. Readers are now more aware of a truth of life as well.

To the degree that readers recognize themselves in Ditto or the other characters, *Breaktime* has succeeded in demonstrating one of those most important values of literature: it is conciliatory, comforting us in our shared humanity, as Chambers has put it in *Introducing Books to Children*. To the degree that readers encounter characters, ideas, or even styles of writing that are alien to their experience, *Breaktime* is subversive, challenging our prejudices and ingrained attitudes. Chambers is learning in this first novel in the "Dance Sequence," as he himself readily admits, how to use his own experiences to capture one kind of truth. The five novels to come ambitiously attempt to capture other truths about being a young person at the end of the twentieth- and the beginning of the twenty-first century.

NOTES

1. Chambers, interview.
2. Chambers, interview.
3. Margery Fisher, *Growing Point* 17.4 (November 1978), 3418.
4. Aidan Chambers, *Breaktime* (New York: Harper, 1978), 16. Hereafter cited in the text.
5. Aidan Chambers, *Introducing Books to Children* (London: Heinemann Educational Books, 1973), 10. Hereafter cited in the text as *Introducing*.
6. Chambers, interview.
7. Geraldine DeLuca, "Taking True Risks: Controversial Issues in New Young Adult Novels," *The Lion and the Unicorn* 3.2 (Winter 1979–80), 135.
8. Richard Yates, "You Can and Can't Go Home Again," *New York Times Book Review* (29 April 1979), 30.
9. Chambers, interview.
10. Yates, 30.
11. Aidan Chambers, *Booktalk: Occasional Writing on Children and Literature* (New York: Harper, 1986), 98.
12. Chambers, *Booktalk*, 98.
13. Chambers, *Booktalk*, 98.
14. Chambers, *Booktalk*, 99.
15. Chambers, *Booktalk*, 106.
16. Chambers, personal website. Retrieved from www.aidanchambers.co.uk/journalism/journalism1.htm. First published as "The Death of Populism" in *The Bookseller* (14 July 2000).
17. Chambers, *Booktalk*, 104.
18. Lauren Adams, "Disorderly Fiction," *Horn Book Magazine* 78.5 (Sep/Oct 2002), 521–29. Academic Search Premier. 25 January 2004. Keyword: Chambers, Aidan.
19. Note that the opening line of *Breaktime* is "Maureen Pinfold is a dream." Not incidentally, her last name is a combination of "centerfold" and "pin-up."
20. Chambers, interview.

Chapter 3

The Flip Side: *Dance on My Grave*

The publishing history of *Dance on My Grave* belies the actual writing history, for this is the only one of Chambers' novels in the Dance Sequence that was begun out of order. Chambers actually began writing this novel in 1966, long before *Breaktime* was thought of, but he didn't get very far with it and put it aside. As he explains, it wasn't until he finished *Breaktime* that he knew how to proceed with that earlier idea: "I wasn't ready for it when the conception happened. I didn't have the technical skills and didn't know myself well enough as a writer. *Breaktime* . . . taught me everything I needed to know."[1] As he thought about picking up *Dance on My Grave* again, after almost twelve years, it occurred to him, he explains, that the novel is a companion piece to *Breaktime*, that "[t]hey share the same thematic concerns, but approach and treat them differently" (*Booktalk*, 111). It was also during the writing of *Dance on My Grave* that Chambers "intuited" that there would be six novels in the sequence.

The conception for the novel came from reading a short news report in *The Guardian* newspaper in 1966. Chambers remembers that it reported the second appearance in juvenile court of a boy accused of desecrating a grave. A social worker reported her findings to the magistrate after interviewing the boy, explaining that the boy had sworn an oath with a friend that if one of them died the other would dance on his grave. They had had an argument over a girl, the other boy had driven off and been killed in an accident, and so the boy had danced on his friend's grave. Chambers notes, however, "What made it odd was that he was caught by a policeman who had been lying in wait behind a nearby gravestone. How did anyone know that the boy was going to dance on the grave? Was this the second time he'd tried? As soon as I read the news item, I felt sure I knew what had actually happened, which the boy had kept secret, and knew that I would write the story as a novel with the title *Dance on My Grave*."[2] It took him twelve years, he says, to find the right form.

Sixteen-year-old Hal Robinson, the boy who does the dancing, meets eighteen-year-old Barry Gorman, the boy whose grave it is, when the former capsizes a sailboat he has borrowed off the coast of Southend-on-Sea, the same English resort town where Chambers took his first teaching job. Barry sails to the rescue on his yellow charger of a sailboat, unconsciously taking on the role of "boy with the magic beans," a concept Hal has gotten from watching a television show when he was seven. In this show, two boys had a series of adventures where they could go back in time because of the magic beans one of the boys had found. In the first of these adventures, the boys swear eternal fealty to one another, to be bosom friends forever, something Hal has longed for all his life. When Barry dies in a motorcycle accident after their intense love affair of only seven weeks, and Hal is arrested for dancing on his grave, Hal must write an account for a social worker charged by the court with recommending a sentence. Hal's journal becomes the novel we read, *Dance on My Grave*.

As even this brief synopsis suggests, the emphasis of the novel is on Hal's response, on his *consciousness*, on what he thinks and feels about what has happened, not on what has happened. As we have seen in *Breaktime*, Chambers writes fiction in which the protagonist becomes intensely interested in how to tell about something so that the telling itself becomes the way to understanding. Along the way, readers come to know his characters intimately and become caught up in their story. His own description of his goals suggests this marriage of form and content that his novels manage to achieve: "I want my fiction to be like 'fact'—what people call 'real life'. Yet at the same time the story is an artefact—a 'fact of art', a made object which is very carefully patterned and crafted."[3] Chambers is, above all, interested in pattern and craft. The subtitle of *Dance on My Grave*, written by the protagonist Hal, demonstrates to what extent Chambers has choreographed this "dance":

The Flip Side: Dance on My Grave

A Life and a Death
in Four Parts
One Hundred and Seventeen Bits
Six Running Reports
and Two Press Clippings
with a few jokes
a puzzle or three
some footnotes
and a fiasco now and then
to help the story along

Examining the pattern of this story shows both how it fits into the larger pattern of the "Dance Sequence" and how it has come to be one of Chambers' most acclaimed novels.

OPPOSITES ATTRACT

Hal is, like Ditto from *Breaktime*, an only child. Perhaps because he is most used to it, he likes to be alone. He also likes to think, which explains why he, a novice sailor who has never taken charge of a boat before, is out alone on a friend's sailboat. He has "borrowed" it, without his friend's knowledge, so that he can have a chance to sit back and think for a while, alone, about his future, which everyone else seems to have strong but conflicting advice about. He's sixteen, a time when the English educational system demands (or did at the time of *Dance on My Grave*) that students choose a career path, whether it is going to include further schooling to train for university or whether it is going to include leaving school for apprenticeship for a job. He is a good writer, as his English teacher Jim Osborn has pointed out, and he's interested in reading. (In this novel the English teacher is actually given the same name as Chambers' own influential teacher.) His school report says he is above average in intelligence, and his linguistic skills certainly show him to be clever. Like Ditto in *Breaktime*, he seems to be smarter than his parents. His mother acknowledges that she and his father can't understand what he is talking about most of the time. His father, however, wants him to do the "practical" thing and get a job—preferably as a baggage handler at the airport, where he works. Hal is torn between these two "fathers"—his biological one and his intellectual one—as his namesake, Prince Hal, is torn in Shakespeare's *Henry IV* between his love of Falstaff, who encourages him in his hell-raising, and his duty as would-be king.

Dance on My Grave makes the connection with Shakespeare explicit. Hal dislikes his real name, Henry, and so decides, in the summer when he meets Barry, as Hal's social worker notes, to change it to Hal. Barry explains to his mother that it's after Prince Hal in Shakespeare's plays *Henry IV* and *Henry V*. Naming of characters is very important in all of Chambers' novels, particularly in *The Toll Bridge*, and so it is interesting that Hal's social worker says he was "cagey" about telling her why he made the change and interesting that Hal doesn't introduce himself to Barry. We hear nothing about his name until Barry explains it to his mother after he and Hal have spent some time together getting Hal bathed and dressed after the capsizing. As throughout the novel, things happen under the surface, are ambiguous and secretive. Did the name change happen in that first meeting with Barry? Exactly when and why was the change made? Did Barry suggest it? We never learn.

However it came about, the name is appropriate. As Prince Hal is in the play, our Hal is young and rather sheltered from the world. He is, he tells us, a "late developer."[4] The social worker says he looks more like fifteen than sixteen. His English teacher agrees that he needs to mature (*Dance*, 65). Shakespeare's Falstaff, that lovable rogue, takes Prince Hal in hand and, depending on your point of view, either leads him astray or "teaches" him the ways of the world. If Hal is like Shakespeare's Prince Hal, the character most like Falstaff is Barry. He is older and leads Hal into bad company—at one point they get mixed up with a gang of bikers—as Falstaff leads Hal into bad company with a number of criminal types. At one point in the play, Falstaff is even likened to the character Vice in medieval morality plays. Barry certainly has a habit of staying out all night and is sexually promiscuous, and he draws Hal into that life.

Unlike Falstaff, however, Barry is enormously attractive and young, but like Falstaff he presents a counterpoint to Hal in many ways. He is everything Hal is not. He is practiced in the ways of the world. He likes people, and people like him. He has, we learn, a habit of picking up people, as his mother suggests when she tells Hal about "all those boys" Barry rescues in his boat, as we see when he refuses to leave the drunk they encounter on their first night together, and as a Norwegian *au pair* tells Hal when she confirms that Barry had sex with her the same day he met her. Unlike Hal, who is a thinker and slow to make up his mind, Barry is impetuous, as we see when he offers Hal a job after knowing him only a few minutes. As Hal is struggling with his journal after Barry dies, trying to be accurate and truthful, he remembers that Barry was a good liar, "lived for the moment," and had no memory because liars don't need them (*Dance*, 113). Above all, he takes risks, as his motorcycle riding, especially his love of speed, suggests: "I never feel I'm going fast. What I feel is that speed is somewhere just ahead, and that I'm chasing it. Always it's just out of reach. So I go faster and faster, trying to catch it" (*Dance*, 131).

Hal and Barry are likened to two other symbolic characters, at least in Hal's mind—David and Jonathan from the Bible. Hal explains that, a few months before he met Barry, his religion teacher read his class a passage "about David (the little guy who gave Goliath the chop with a sling stone) and Jonathan (the tearaway son of fierce King Saul)." Hal continues, "David and Jonathan got a thing going between them, apparently, because they started talking about the soul of Jonathan being knit with the soul of David, and Jonathan loving David as his own soul. . . . I found myself sitting up and taking notice just like I had all those years ago in front of the telly" (*Dance*, 51–52). Hal is remembering the television series that had had such a profound effect on him when he was seven, in which two boys swear eternal fealty to each other as bosom friends. But here, Hal says, was meat far more nourishing for a sixteen-year-old than those magic beans one of the television characters found.

Hal is so intrigued by this passage that he looks up the whole story for himself in the Book of Samuel and finds David crying out at the death of Jonathan, "Thy love to me was wonderful, passing the love of women." Hal notes that the Bible never goes into too much detail, so he was left to wonder what it meant, "and, more importantly, what exactly had happened between them to make David think like that. For God's sake, what had they *done* to—with?—each other? . . . One thing was sure. David and Jonathan were archetypal bosom friends. No question" (*Dance*, 52). Hal has been trying to use his journal to sort out his feelings for Barry and to try to explain why he felt them. As he catalogues his past search for the "bosom friend" and why all the candidates fell short, it becomes clear, to him and to us, that there is a sexual element in Hal's search. He has known since he was fourteen that he was homosexual, and he has known that there has been something missing in his relationships with his past "bosom pals." David and Jonathan have convinced him that what he has been looking for includes a sexual relationship. When he is rescued by Barry, he finds his Jonathan (the tearaway son) for his David (the little guy).

A KIND OF LOVE

Although the novel is quite open and matter-of-fact about the main characters' homosexuality—no concessions in content, as Chambers decided early on—homosexuality never becomes an *issue* to be dealt with. A review in *The Horn Book* makes the point that many critics did when the book was released: "A major strength of the book, the central conflict hinges not on the lovers being gay, but on their having two idiosyncratic and contradictory personalities."[5] That central conflict is the *obsessive* love that Hal has for Barry. As he looks back in his journal, Hal writes, "I couldn't get enough of him. I wanted to be with him all the time. And yet when I was with him that wasn't enough either. I wanted to look at him and touch him and have him touch me and hear him talk and tell him things and do things together with him. All the time. Day and night. For 4,233,600 seconds [the time Hal has worked out that he had with Barry before his death]" (*Dance*, 155). But as Hal finds out, Barry doesn't feel the same way.

The argument that leads to Barry's death is ultimately not about his behavior with a girl he meets. He has taken the Norwegian *au pair* that he and Hal meet on the beach to bed with him on the first night they know each other, and Hal is furiously jealous. Barry explains his behavior by saying, "We've had a few laughs, sure. Had a good time. But I like a change now and then. More than that really. I want to get into as many different things as I can . . . [chuckling] as many different people. One is never enough. Not for me." It goes even deeper than this, though. Barry has realized something that Hal hasn't, an essential difference between them. He goes on, "I thought you wanted the same things I do. . . . But that's not you, is it? It's not what we do together that you want. It's me. All of me. All for yourself. And that's too heavy for me, Hal. I don't want to be owned, and I don't want to be sucked dry. Not by anyone. Ever" (*Dance*, 179). The essential difference is between two very different kinds of love.

Although homosexuality is not the issue—obsessive love is—*Dance on My Grave* has been criticized for its portrayal of gay sex, not because it celebrates gay pleasure but because it focuses on pain. In a chapter about sexuality in her book *Disturbing the Universe: Power and Repression in Adolescent Literature*, Roberta Trites praises both *Breaktime* and *Dance on My Grave* for their open treatment of sexuality that never devolves into didacticism. In *Breaktime*, she argues, "Aidan Chambers is unusual in depicting a heterosexual scene from a male perspective that allows for female sexual agency." Both Ditto and Helen have enjoyed their shared sexual experience, and "neither ends up diseased, pregnant, emotionally devastated, or dead."[6] And in *Dance on My Grave*, Trites concedes, sex with Barry does bring Hal physical and emotional pleasure. The book is "emphatically not" the typical problem novel, in that "[b]eing gay is not Hal Robinson's problem . . . ; grief over the death of Barry Gorman, Hal's lover, is."[7] However, even though the novel communicates that "obsessive love is not healthy, regardless of one's sexual orientation," it also contains, Trites argues, "an almost Calvinistic series of messages about homosexuality" and also conforms to the standard stereotypes in adolescent novels about gay males: both gay characters are white, middle-class, single children; one's mother is terrifically overbearing and said to have an "overactive Id"; Hal is forced to dress as a girl to view his lover's body; he is denied a photograph of his lover; he is arrested for fulfilling an oath to his lover; and, "worst of all," his father "almost certainly perceives his sexual orientation as pathological," Trites concludes.[8] So while Chambers is affirmative about being gay, she finds it unfortunate that the novel focuses more on Hal's pain than on his pleasure.

THE FLIP SIDE OF *BREAKTIME*

Trites is correct in noting the novel's focus, also that it simply reflects what it meant to be gay in the 1980s. But her book doesn't point out that *Dance on My Grave*'s role as companion book to *Breaktime* demands this focus. Chambers explains his conception of the two books in an interesting architectural metaphor: "In *Breaktime* all the workings are on show, as all the innards of the Pompidou building in Paris are on show. It is heterosexual, masculine, plain-speaking, revelatory. In *Dance on My Grave* all the workings are hidden, as they are hidden in the walls of, say, a Georgian building, or are inside and under the floorboards. It is homosexual, feminine, ambiguous, aware that nothing ever means only one thing" (*Booktalk*, 111).

One of the most obvious ways that the two books differ, as both Trites and Chambers point out, is in their treatments of sex. *Breaktime* has as an important final scene: the attempt to convey, in some detail, the experience of the sex act in its wholeness—both the mental and the physical experience. In doing so, it is graphic. *Dance on My Grave*, on the other hand, only alludes to sex acts, although it is clear what is taking place. They are never described. Trites suggests that this reticence is due to publishing codes at the time, but it has much more to do with the structure of the book as a whole. Hal talks in riddles, sometimes cagey, often in comic ones. Such ambiguous telling is demanded by two important features, his audience and his consciousness.

As the reader finds out two-thirds through the novel, the "you" that Hal addresses in the book is Ms. Atkins, his social worker. In an attempt to convince Jim Osborn to help her with her investigation of what happened, she tells him that the court will send Hal to a Detention Center unless she can find out the truth. Knowing that this course of action would be disastrous for Hal, but also not wishing to betray Hal's confidence, Osborn agrees to do everything he can to convince Hal to tell her himself, if she will in turn promise to recommend to the court that Hal be allowed to return to school. So the fact that Hal is writing to his social worker demands a degree of reticence in the telling. But Osborn also explains to the social worker that it is important for Hal to verbalize what happened with Barry *for his own sake*. Her report explains, "[Jim Osborn] felt that Hal was brooding on it all, and that this was bad for him, and might have worse long term effects than any treatment the court might impose on him" (*Dance*, 125). In large part, then, Hal is addressing himself, struggling to understand what he himself doesn't understand and frustrated because "the words don't say what I want them to say" (*Dance*, 164). Therefore, he doesn't go into more detail about his sexual experiences both because he doesn't want to remember, or can't, as he says he can't remember Barry's face after he dies, and also because *Hal* knows what these experiences were and sees no need to detail them.

The more relevant reason for his reticence, however, is the nature of his consciousness, his state of being. Hal's is the voice we hear.

Therefore, Chambers must reproduce what it is like to be Hal, just as he reproduced in *Breaktime* what it is like to be Ditto. Hal is obsessed, not only with Barry—as he was in life and as he is in death—but with words, images, symbols, with their ability or lack of ability to create understanding, and he is obsessed with his desperate need to understand. In that same essay, "Ways of Telling," in which Chambers discusses the "geology" of *Breaktime*, he offers an important key to Hal, that Hal's writing tends to be as secretive as it is revelatory. So, for example, Hal's social worker notes that when she first meets Hal he avoided questions he didn't like by giving flippant replies. Similarly, he writes in his journal of the first time he and Barry have sex: "[Barry] gave me a present from Southend. Wish you were here?" (*Dance*, 149). He uses that euphemism most often, funny and at the same time secretive. He says that Barry gave him lots of kinds of presents that he hadn't had before. For one, he uses the slang expression "plate of ham" for fellatio. As the social worker notes, Hal is cagey.

AMBIGUOUS, AMBIVALENT, ARTISTIC

Hal is also well read, and to try to convey his thoughts and feelings he makes a number of references to the arts, both literary and visual. The center of this novel is Kurt Vonnegut, as James Joyce was the center of *Breaktime*. The epigraph to Part I is a quotation from Vonnegut's own introduction to his novel *Mother Night*, about an American spy in WW II whose cover was as a broadcaster of Nazi propaganda. He played the role so successfully that now he is being hunted as a war criminal. Vonnegut claimed in the introduction that of all his books this was the only one whose moral was clear to him: "We are what we pretend to be, so we must be careful what we pretend to be," the epigraph Hal uses. In that first section, Hal admits that when he first sees Barry coming to rescue him from the sea, he goes into a "lost-and-hopeless-kid routine" and can almost feel himself performing, acting the part. He wants Barry to feel competent, and he wants to put himself into Barry's hands completely. In the remainder of their time together, then, Hal is the kid, the student, the victim in the relationship. He wears what Barry tells him to wear, and he does what Barry tells him to do. Until, that is, Barry gets tired of the game, as Kari, the Norwegian *au pair*, tries to explain to Hal:

"For a while, I'd guess, Barry enjoyed you depending on him like that. Enjoyed being your teacher, showing you about life, about yourself. I think he got a thrill out of playing your big brother, and your lover, and your boss, and your guru all at the same time. But, being Barry, he'd get tired of it after a while, because what he liked most was the beginnings of things" (*Dance*, 245). So Barry yells at Hal, in their final argument, "You Bore Me!" (*Dance*, 178).

Like Vonnegut's *Mother Night*, *Dance on My Grave* explores the dichotomy between appearance and truth, between perception and identity, and between what people are and what we want them to be. As Hal says at the end, after he has finished his journal, we invent the people we know. In the same way, Vonnegut says, we invent ourselves.

Hal also quotes from John Donne. The epigraph to Part II is from Donne's elegy "The Perfume": "Once, and but once found in thy company, / All thy supposed escapes are laid on me." Donne is talking here to his wife-to-be of her parents' desperate attempts to discover whether she is having sex before her wedding. However, Donne is the one her parents blame for all her "supposed escapes," her misbehavior, when she is actually as impatient as he is. (Note the similarity to *Breaktime* and its grounding in the Shakespearean comic plot of youth impatient to declare their independence and be free of the old guard.) Hal sees a connection between his situation and Donne's in that Barry is the one doing the misbehaving but Hal is the one blamed. Part II contains Hal's accounts of their first night together when Barry refuses to leave a drunk man they happen to encounter because, Hal concludes, Barry is incapable of "resisting temptation." Barry obviously has sex with the man after Hal leaves, yet Hal is blamed by Barry's mother for keeping him out so late. The section also contains the scene in which Barry takes Hal for his first motorcycle ride and gets them involved with a gang of bikers in the Southend Fun Fair, ending in a street fight where they both get beat up. That night concludes with Hal's first "present from Southend" and his swearing the oath that Barry insists on—"Whichever of us dies first, the other promises to dance on his grave" (*Dance*, 151). The four parts of the novel, like the four parts of *Breaktime*, are like four acts of a play; in the exact center is the oath, because, Hal says, "At that moment there was nothing I wouldn't have done for him" (*Dance*, 152). Barry is clearly the cause of the trouble Hal finds himself in, both legally and emotionally.

Barry also makes references to literature and art, but in his case to important homosexual artists: David Hockney, the painter, and W. H. Auden, the poet. The reader learns from these references clues to Barry's personality—he is knowledgeable and cultured, and he also was asked, like Hal, to join Jim Osborn's hand-picked circle of English literature students before he left school to take over his parents' record shop when his father died. To Hal, Barry also looks like one of the people in a Hockney painting, which he has on his bedroom wall: "All part of an arrangement, like a still-life, a little too posed for real life, very clean, bright, clear-cut, airy. I liked their sharp-focus quality, and the feeling that there was something elusive, something waiting behind all that studied informality" (*Dance*, 37). Hal feels the same elusive quality when Barry quotes an Auden poem when they wake in bed: "Lay your sleeping head, my love, / Human on my faithless arm." Barry is able to explain that, "by strange coincidence," the author's initials, W. H., are the same as those of the person to whom Shakespeare dedicated his sonnets, "widely thought to have been his boyfriend" (*Dance*, 158). Auden's poem calls those that lie in his arms "guilty," a concept about homosexuality that Hal is surprised both Auden and Barry seem to accept, at least here. *Dance on My Grave* depends on such elusiveness. As Chambers has said of the novel, it is "aware that nothing ever means only one thing" (*Booktalk*, 111).

Part of the novel's elusiveness is communicated by symbolic images. Chambers himself calls attention to many of these in his essay "Ways of Telling": the sea, mirrors, helmets, pictures, gifts, "clothes of one kind and another and what dressing in them means" (*Booktalk*, 112). For example, Hal is "capsized" when he is found by Barry, literally and figuratively, "at sea" and in an upheaval. In that first encounter, so much is going on "under the surface" as they both are aware of a sexual tension, a pun Hal himself makes about "the seaborne nature" of their meeting (*Dance*, 53). In another example, Hal is continually looking in a mirror—in the Gormans' bathroom as he takes a bath there after he capsizes, trying to see whether his knees are attractive through Barry's eyes, as he dresses in girls' clothes so he can sneak into the morgue and see Barry's body, and, finally, when he throws the paperweight at Barry's head and shatters the mirror holding his own image, his face falling in splinters to the floor. Barry, too, is continually looking in a mirror. Again, there is a similarity to Conrad's *The Secret Sharer*, as discussed in chapter two in relation to *Breaktime*, both in the sea and in the mirror images.

The sea rescue is the same as in Conrad's short story, but the roles are reversed. That is, Barry is doing the rescuing of the young, inexperienced one, but he is actually the secret sharer that Hal has been looking for all his life. The whole point of bosom buddies is that you get someone who is the other half, as a bosom is made up of two breasts. And as the secret sharer in Conrad's story is the young captain's doppelganger, or other half, so Barry is Hal's, but he is the dark, scary side, and the self-destructive side, as symbolized in the final shattering of the mirror (as the secret sharer, a murderer, is the young captain's dark side). That is why Hal is frightened when he thinks of Barry. Doppelgangers are nothing more than human mirrors. Like Narcissus looking into the reflecting pool and falling in love with his own image, Barry and Hal both look into mirrors and fall in love with what they see, the image of what they want to be reflected back. Barry dresses Hal in his own image, and Hal wears the clothes for a time, happy to reflect Barry. Until the mirror shatters. "We are what we pretend to be, so we must be careful what we pretend to be," as Vonnegut says. Reality and illusion are easily mixed up, Chambers reminds us, here and also in *Breaktime*.

As Joseph Conrad is important to both *Breaktime* and *Dance on My Grave*, so is James Joyce, in this novel in an extended symbolic scene that also calls attention to the fluid nature of reality and illusion. Chambers has said that the details of the scene where Hal and Barry get mixed up with a gang of bikers are taken from a maturational dream described and analyzed by Carl Jung in *Man and His Symbols* (*Booktalk*, 112). This scene is indeed nightmarish, as is the Nighttown episode in *Ulysses*, in which both of the main characters, Leopold Bloom and the younger Stephen Dedalus, visit the red-light district of Dublin. Both the action and the telling of this chapter of *Ulysses*, alternating between naturalistic description and hallucinatory fantasy, resemble the scene in the fun-fair with the bikers in *Dance on My Grave*. In both, the young, innocent one is taken by an older person and shown the darker side of life; in both, there is a fight and a rescue. The motorcycle Barry and Hal are riding is surrounded by a group of bikers, and they are swept along, with Barry's help, into the nightmarish world of the Southend fun-fair. When their pretense of being foreigners is discovered, they are embroiled in a fight with the gang and only survive because they are helped by a friend of Hal's.

Jung describes a typical initiation scene in his maturation dream, where innocence is given some experience. Shakespeare, too, casts

Falstaff and Prince Hal in the roles of teacher and student, initiator and initiated, where Prince Hal learns important lessons about his subjects-to-be and about the seamy side of life from Falstaff. Leopold Bloom similarly initiates Stephen in *Ulysses*. Joyce knew Jung's work well, especially since Jung was for a time psychoanalyst of Joyce's daughter, and both he and Conrad in "The Secret Sharer" make use of Jung's concept of the "night journey," the voyage into the unconscious that is necessary for self-knowledge. Chambers calls on both Joyce and Jung, as well as Conrad and Shakespeare, as we have seen. Hal is "initiated" by Barry in this scene, into the darker side of life represented by the bikers and into sexual experience, for Hal gets his first "present from Southend" at the end of this night. All of the novels in the "Dance Sequence" explore what it means to be young and inexperienced, just as they all remind us that a person is not one thing but has many sides, a concept Chambers will explore more fully in *NIK: Now I Know* and *The Toll Bridge*.

FORMAL TECHNIQUES

All of the novels in the "Dance Sequence" also use complex forms to try to reproduce the experience of the main characters, what Chambers calls "ways of telling our experience" (*Booktalk*, 112). Both he and Hal, Chambers says, struggle with certain questions: "How do I tell about what happened so that it makes sense? How do I tell it so that the telling is true about what happened then but is also true about what is happening now? How is the past turned into the present? How is memory made into meaning?" (*Booktalk*, 113). As Chambers points out, the entire book is about memory and the shifting effects of memory—what Hal was feeling *then* and what he is feeling *now*.

In this novel, the narrative solution to this problem most often used is that of the television instant replay, commonly seen in sports programs. Chambers' description perfectly captures the television viewer's experience (he is describing a soccer game but the experience is the same for American football):

> Even as a game of football is in progress, the viewer is shown the action replay of a goal that was scored a few seconds before. The replay will be shown in slow-motion so that we can see whether the goal was offside, say, or a player was fouled or not, even while the referee is still

arguing the point with players on the field. And while the slow-motion replay is being shown the unseen presenters give a voice-over commentary in which they remark on the way the goal was scored. That is, they recuperate for us the meaning and significance of the event. They act as a kind of narrator. Of course, if the producer wants to s/he can also use split-screen. Part of the picture will show us the action replay, the other part will show the game as it continues (the referee arguing with the players and then the play starting again). If this is done, we are watching the real present of the game—the game's story as it happens—and the historic present of the goal being scored—the game's immediate past recalled—both at the same time. And when we view these two time-scales together, and simultaneously hear the presenters' discussion of the events, our feelings about the game change, and our view of the real present of the game as it continues changes. We have a different view of the game, and different views about it, from those who are actually there and cannot watch as we watch. (*Booktalk*, 113).

Chambers was so struck by the experience of watching these instant replays, he says, that he uses them as a narrative device in *Dance on My Grave*.

So, for example, the capsizing of the boat Hal is in is described first, dispassionately, complete with diagrams. Immediately following, however, is the action replay of the capsizing, a slow-motion version of the event, now with Hal's commentary. He tells us that everything happened in a couple of seconds, but "from the moment I make my mistake with the tiller to the moment when I scramble on to the sloughing hull, everything seems to take place out of time." He continues, "I see now . . . ," so the reader is able to contemplate the event again as Hal contemplates it. Similarly, the fight between the motorcycle gang and Hal and Barry is slowed down with an instant replay, allowing readers to focus on what it felt like to Hal to be in the fight rather than on the exciting "what happens next." In this example, readers see the flip side of the fight in *Breaktime*, which as Chambers points out is given the opposite treatment—it is shown in fast-motion, no commentary at all, just a cartoon drawing of a fist. A slow-motion instant replay is also used when Hal is caught by the guard as he tries to sneak into the mortuary dressed as a girl to see Barry's body. Hal keeps replaying his "mental video," as he calls it, and "[e]ach time the me that is me detached a little more the me that was me from the me that is me." (*Dance*, 101).

The result of all these instant replays is very metafictional; that is, they call the reader's attention to the *writing*. At one point Hal says that a pause in his mother's conversation was "as long as this page" (*Dance*, 109). Later Hal tells us that it took him three days to write the account of the morgue, but that "I have become my own character. I as I was, not I as I am now. Put another way: Because of writing this story, I am no longer now what I was when it all happened. Writing the story is what has changed me; not having lived through the story" (*Dance*, 221). The form of the story has taken center stage, rather than the plot.

A similar effect is achieved by the technique of Hal's "corrections." After he writes something, he often stops himself to add a correction, for, he says, he wouldn't bother writing his journal in the first place unless he tries to "get it right" (*Dance*, 42). So, for example, he says about his first meeting with Barry, "That was how it was. *Correction*: That was how it was not. We said all that. But there was more going on behind our faces so to speak" (*Dance*, 42). When Barry meets the Norwegian *au pair* who precipitates the final argument that leads to his death, Hal writes, "That, as nearly as I can remember, was how the conversation went, how the end began. Because that is the trouble—*Correction*: That is part of the trouble—I can't remember so much about the end" (*Dance*, 172–73). Chambers achieves the same effect that Henry James does in a novel such as *The Golden Bowl* in which the story of the four principal characters is continually broken in on by the couple who has observed the action and now is telling it, but with the disagreements common to human beings with imperfect memories: "Don't you remember, this is the way it happened, not as you said" or "No, I'm sure she said it this way." How the story is told *is* the story.

SHAKESPEAREAN PATTERNS

Memory is the story, as it is in *Hamlet*, the play Barry and Hal go to see together. Barry is clearly affected by the play, and he tries to explain the reason to Hal. He says, "The remembering is what is so hard." The ghost of Hamlet's father tells him "Remember me," but Hamlet can't—"That's why he feels so guilty. Why he wears his father's picture around his neck: to remind him. Why he forces his mother to look at it. He says his mother has forgotten his father. But he's talking about himself really. It's his own guilt that's driving him mad, not his mother shacking up with his uncle."⁹ Hal figures out that Barry is thinking of the death of his own father when he says that you can't remember anymore and think that you should—you can't recall the face and you feel guilty. After Barry dies, Hal feels equally guilty. That's why he has migraines, why he becomes obsessed with getting a photograph of Barry and with seeing his dead body. Why he says over and over that he can't recall Barry's face. Why he concludes that he is mad, in the same way Hamlet is mad.

Here Shakespeare is an explicit reference, as it is when Barry explains that Shakespeare's sonnets were addressed to "W. H.," but Chambers' interest in all things Shakespearean underpins *Dance on My Grave* in the same way that the pattern of the characteristic Shakespearean comic plot, "Young people in rebellion against waning adult authority," underpins *Breaktime* (*Booktalk*, 98). The story of *Dance on My Grave*, Chambers points out, is really a rather banal love story if cast in the usual boy-girl terms. It has a beginning and end but very little in the middle. But cast in boy-boy terms, the story is changed at once: "It's looked at differently, it's thought about differently, and it has a different effect," Chambers notes. He goes on, "Shakespeare plays at that game all the time, and it wasn't only because they didn't have female actors. It wasn't only that." Chambers' reading in the literature of that time has convinced him, he says, that male love and bisexuality were deeply ingrained in Elizabethan culture, and it certainly was a feature on the stage. "I was actually taught, even by Jim Osborn, that there would have been no kissing on the stage. We know without any doubt that there was because some of the Puritans were complaining that going to see the plays in the theatre inflamed men's passion for boys. And where Shakespeare has a kiss, it's given as a stage direction in the first folio. So it was going on. And the audience liked that—it's part of that whole time." Chambers argues that such gender issues are an important part of this time, too.[10] As in Shakespeare's plays, such "gender bending" goes "deep" in all the novels in the "Dance Sequence."

NO ENDINGS

Hal writes in his last journal entry that "I wouldn't want you to think that this is the end." What he has come to understand is that there are no endings. Hal no longer thinks in terms of endings. Maybe what he has written in his journal is just the beginning. Maybe not even that. It is "just a bit of the middle of something that has a beginning and an end so far out of sight you might as well forget about them, as if they weren't there at all, which they aren't when you come to think about it" (*Dance*, 252). And of course, Aidan Chambers doesn't think in terms of endings either. As his biography shows, there is always a new episode, always a new beginning. None of his writing, he says, "is ever an end in itself or ever comes to an end. None of it is self-contained. . . . All of it belongs, I hope and believe, to a continuum that cannot have an end" (*Booktalk*, 115). That continuum includes the Bible, Shakespeare, Donne, Eliot, Auden, Vonnegut—all the writers and all the works that are a part of *Dance on My Grave* and that *Dance on My Grave* is a part of.

NOTES

1. Chambers, personal website. Retrieved from www.aidanchambers.co.uk/faqs.htm.
2. Chambers, e-mail correspondence, 16 January 2005.
3. Chambers, personal website. Retrieved from www.aidanchambers.co.uk/faqs.htm.
4. Aidan Chambers, *Dance on My Grave* (New York: Harper, 1982), 43. Hereafter cited in the text as *Dance*.
5. Gregory Maquire, *The Horn Book Magazine* 59.3 (1983), 308.
6. Roberta Trites, *Disturbing the Universe: Power and Repression in Young Adult Literature* (Iowa City: University of Iowa Press, 2000), 97.
7. Trites, 104–5.
8. Trites, 106–7.
9. It is interesting that Joyce's Nighttown episode in *Ulysses* also includes appearances by the ghost of Bloom's father and the ghost of Stephen's mother.
10. Chambers, personal interview.

Chapter 4

A Canticle of Faith: *NIK: Now I Know*

Aidan Chambers began to write the novel that was to become *NIK: Now I Know* (published as *Now I Know* in Britain) in 1983, a year after he finished *Dance on My Grave*. Normally he had already started thinking about his next novel while he was finishing the one before, but *Dance*, he says, "wore me out. It took me a year to recover from that."[1] In that year he was looking around to see where the next book was coming from, for he believes that every book has to be found—it can't be forced. *Breaktime* and *Dance on My Grave* seemed like a pair to him; only then did he sense that "there were elements missing if I could have written a great big book about the nature of adolescence." Only then did a pattern of six books start to appear and it became clear to him that certain topics would have to be dealt with, "but which order that dealing would come" he didn't know, couldn't have said number 3 will be like this and number 4 will be like that.[2]

He calls it "serendipity," a happy accident, that he found *NIK*. Like *Dance on My Grave*, which also began with a short piece Chambers read, *Now I Know* has its origins in a short passage in a book he was reading at the time, *The Book of Laughter and Forgetting* by Czech author Milan Kundera, an unusual collection of seven interrelated stories that are part fiction, part autobiography, and part philosophical treatise. Chambers says he was inexplicably struck by a passage about the protagonist's old father, who is trying to play Beethoven's Sonata 111: "In the passage the old man suddenly stabs his finger again and again at the score, saying 'Now I know! Now I know!' I cannot explain why this meant so much to me at the time. But it hit me with the power of revelation, and I knew at once I'd found the next book in the sequence, that it would tackle the nature of rational thought as against irrational belief, and that the central character would be a boy called Nik."[3] Although there is a brief sentence in *Dance on My Grave* where Jim Osborn, Hal's teacher, tells him, "If you go on like this you'll turn religious, you know that, don't you," Chambers now is amused to find that the book seemed to know something he didn't know himself: "Sometimes your books know where you're going, or where they're taking you, a long time before you know yourself" (*Booktalk*, 115). His next book would be about spirituality.

A teenager's spiritual life is a subject not often tackled in a novel. Chambers says that when he was writing his early novels the subject was "almost taboo, nobody talked about it." And so, like the subject of sex, which is so essential to the thoughts and actions of teenagers but which was often ignored in novels of the '60s and '70s designed to be read by them, Chambers determined that spirituality was one of the subjects that had to be dealt with in a sequence of novels attempting to explore the nature of adolescent experience at the turn of the twenty-first century. "You can't miss it out."[4] He was also ready to revisit the seven years he had spent in the monastery. It had been fifteen years since he had left it, and, he says, "I had ignored it until then. I knew I had to face that."[5] So in Chambers' third novel in the "Dance Sequence," *NIK: Now I Know*, there are three characters in three interrelated stories, all involved in an aspect of Christian faith, all looking for Jesus, but in three very different ways.

Seventeen-year-old Nik Frome has been strong-armed by his history teacher into being researcher for a film group making a movie about what would happen if Jesus returned to the world today. Nik, an atheist and rational skeptic with a scientific mind, goes looking for the historical Jesus, but he is actually on a quest to discover what it feels like to believe. He wants to understand faith. As part of his research he attends a Christian peace rally, where he meets and falls for Julie, an older girl committed to her faith but still on a quest to discover the particular relationship she is going to have with Jesus. The feelings Nik and Julie have for each other complicate each of their quests, as does the terrorist bomb that severely injures Julie shortly after she has rejected Nik's tentative sexual advances. The third character, a young police detective, is on a much more straightforward quest: someone was seen in a junkyard hanging from some iron made into a cross, and he needs to find out who it was and who did it. He is on a quest to discover who this modern-day Jesus is, victim of a modern-day crucifixion. These three threads weave in and out of a story told through Nik's notebooks, Julie's letters to Nik dictated from her hospital bed, straightforward narrative, commentary and "stockshots" intercut in the manner of a film script, quotations from a number of literary works, and "word clusters" that are not quite poetry and not quite prose.

NIK: Now I Know is Chambers' most philosophical novel, but it has the same concerns with language and form, with how to tell and, in telling, how to understand, as do the other novels in the "Dance Sequence." Here, though, narrative and linguistic patterns become even more intricate, a dance in which readers must participate if they are to make sense of the complexities. As Nik says in his notebook, "Making the connections is what matters."[6]

NIK THE SOLOIST

Like Ditto in *Breaktime* and Hal in *Dance on My Grave*, Nik is an only child. He is also a loner, even more than they are. He knows that other students look down on him for not being part of a group, and so he openly scorns them: "In self-protection, and out of cussed principle, he had encouraged this view of himself as an oddity, making an aggressive virtue of being an outsider" (*NIK*, 17). However, he finds himself quite ironically looked up to by a group of students who admire his aloofness and try to imitate it. This group is even given a name, the Nikelodeons, shortened to the Nikies, shortened to the Niks. He secretly enjoys his status, though, because as he notes there is one great disadvantage to being a loner, and that is being alone all the time. The reader learns that Nik is not antisocial; he simply is uncomfortable with large groups. He occasionally would like some company; in fact, he has recently had a violent physical reaction to a realization of his separateness. He was upset not because he realized that he will die, but because he feels no connection to any other human being. This knowledge about himself predisposes him to become a part of a film group and to become attached to a girl who is very comfortable with herself, with both her aloneness and her connection to Jesus.

Nik is also smart, like both Ditto and Hal. He is singled out by his history teacher to be the researcher for the film group because he is one of the better students, and the incentive is that he will be allowed to submit his findings for part of his exam assessment work. Nik is at first reluctant. He has all the negative feelings about religion that Chambers says he had when he was Nik's age. When his teacher argues that the subject would make a perfect history project because "God has been around a long time," Nik counters, smirking, "God has never been around at all. He's an invention. God's a fiction, sir. Just a story. In the past people needed some all powerful being to explain things they couldn't understand, and to calm their fears. Or to blame for the awful things that happened to them, like illnesses and earthquakes. . . . But we know better now" (*NIK*, 12–13). Nik further argues that he wants nothing to do with religion because of all the hate and torture and wars that have been perpetrated in its name. He is a thinker, though, and agrees to do the project. His teacher has talked him into it with the logical argument that historians simply tell the story of people and how they got to be the way they are, by studying the forces that act on people; they don't take sides or proselytize. That's what *NIK: Now I Know* is going to do. Readers are surprised to find that a book about religion is in no way evangelical.

CHAMBERS' EXPERIENCE AS MONK

Readers are even more surprised to find that a book about religion *by an ex-monk* is completely devoid of any evangelicalism, or indeed any evangelical characters. A review in the *Times Literary Supplement* perfectly expresses such an authorial stance, remarking that there is "never an assertion of values, let alone truth." The novel shows "zeal for integrity," it concludes, "not salvation."[7] Chambers' experiences both before and during his seven years in an Anglican monastery help explain such an attitude and an approach. Chambers' own youth was very much like Nik's in terms of skepticism toward religion. It was also like Nik's in terms of intellectual curiosity. As a student in high school and college, Chambers recounts, "the usual thing" was to have long, philosophical discussions: "One of those subjects that kept coming up was religion. I was violently antireligion; most of us were, I think." Even when he took his first job as a teacher in Southend-on-Sea, he continued to hold these negative feelings about religion, despite the fact that he was surrounded by practicing Christians—nine of the eleven other new teachers—an odd circumstance, Chambers admits. As the philosophical discussions continued, since they were all bachelors and "lived school," Chambers laughs, the others began to "beat me into a corner, intellectually." How could he talk about religion when he had never experienced it, they argued, similar to the argument Nik's teacher makes to him: religion has been a powerful force in history, so anyone who claims to have a thoughtful and inquisitive mind must enter into it in order to understand it. The monastery also had a strong appeal for someone of Chambers' temperament, as also becomes true of Nik. To someone who needs solitude and quiet but also a connection to other human beings with similar goals, someone who needs time for quiet reflection but also the built-in sharing with others of a similar temperament, monastic life is enormously attractive. Finally, both Chambers and Nik had the added incentive of the attraction of something totally new, something people they were attracted to believed deeply but which they "preached" only by the example of their lives. They never tried to convert others.[8]

JULIE THE SOLOIST

Nik's attraction is to Julie, or at least to her life. The reader meets her first through her letters dictated to Nik from her hospital bed, after a bomb blast has severely injured her. Therefore, what is forefronted is her personality, and what she is searching for—not what Nik thinks she is or what she is to him. The reader hears her questioning: "I've been trying to think about what pain *means*. Why do we have to have it? Why do people suffer?" (*NIK*, 39). Her question is the same as the one explored by Christian writer C. S. Lewis, whose major work is called *The Problem of Pain*. That is to be one answer she is searching for throughout: why has she been chosen, like Jesus, to suffer? But her ultimate question concerns what her role in life is to be. As Nik notices about Julie, "She's convinced, but unsure." That is, she is secure in her Christian faith, but that is no cause for her to be complacent. She is still asking questions. After she explains to Nik why she was so silent when she took him to church for the first time—because she was thinking about the Gospel for the day, the Feeding of the Four Thousand—Nik is taken with her manner. She is not preachy, not trying to convert him, just "[t]rying to sort out something for herself. . . . It isn't that she doubts, but that she isn't satisfied that she's got it right yet. She's a believer who you feel won't be happy—no, that's wrong . . . who won't be *content* till she's solved a vast, complicated mystery. And she's working at it all the time" (*NIK*, 98).

Nik asks her why she is a Christian if she condemns what Christian countries do, for she has become incensed by the difference between the sharing in the Gospel story and the way "Christian" countries "hang on to the spare food we've got, while other people starve." She explains to him both her belief and why she does what she does: "You can't put anything right by abandoning it. . . . God didn't think we were beyond redemption, so she joined in and dirtied her hands in order to help put things right. That's what the story of Christ is all about. And so that's the least I can do" (*NIK*, 96–97). Julie calls God "she" because, as she explains, "If God is everything, that must mean God is a she as well as a he, mustn't it? So if you call God he, I don't see why I shouldn't call her she" (*NIK*, 82).

Julie does get her hands dirty. She is injured, but it's important *how* she is injured. If it is only important to the novel that she suffer great pain and be in a hospital dictating letters to a faraway Nik, the more usual way—the way readers would accept as more believable perhaps—would be a car accident or some other everyday occurrence. But Julie is injured as she runs, in great distress and great outrage, to help a man lying wounded in a street next to a car that has exploded. The police are holding back the crowd of onlookers because they are afraid that the man might be the bomber himself and that there might be a second explosion. No one is helping him, so Julie—in Good Samaritan fashion—runs past the police line. As she reaches him with outstretched hands, "as if toward a lover," the second explosion goes off. Julie is injured sacrificing her own safety while trying to help another, doing something Christlike. Her good is contrasted with the terrorist's evil.

When *NIK: Now I Know* was written, explosions by Irish Republican Army bombs were common in England. The Mideast was also constantly rocked by bombs, as it still is today. Since then, of course, we have seen many more bombs, on our own soil and all over the world, in the name of many different causes. No one claims responsibility for the bomb that injures Julie. The evil is random and anonymous. But she is not bitter. She actually understands why terrorists do what they do, that it is a protest against the way we live and a desire for change, although she thinks it is rather childish to try to do something dramatic so that people will pay attention to you, like kids making big banging noises when they are little and startling the grown-ups. But Julie comes to the conclusion, because of her intimate experience with bombs, that, as much as she might want change, she will never do anything that will make things worse for somebody else. Also, she loves life too much, even though it is just a "waiting room"; getting on with her journey, keeping herself fit for it, is necessary if she is to reach her destination (*NIK*, 174–78).

Because of that determination, that assurance, that dedication, Nik is drawn to her from the moment he sees her at the Christian peace rally. He is struck, even at a distance, by Julie's energy but even more by her wholeness. He tries to describe what he sees and feels in his notebook afterwards. Unlike the others, who were only playing at being demonstrators, Julie was in a group but "wasn't being anything but herself. You could tell she *meant* it. Felt it. Her thoughts were her own. I mean were part of her" (*NIK*, 57). Nik seems almost to envy her.

A SHIFT TOWARD THE FEMININE

When Chambers discusses the six novels that make up the "Dance Sequence," he describes a pattern that he says was at first intuitive and then became conscious, which is his usual way of working: In the six novels there is a gradual shift toward the feminine. Everything Chambers wrote before these novels he describes as very male-centered, very chauvinistic in fact. Even *Breaktime*, he notes, is totally masculine. "The pattern of those six novels," Chambers says, "taken in the order in which they were written . . . , in those novels the girl occupies more and more of the books, either in the content of the stories or in the telling of them. . . . By the third book I knew what was happening because the patterns, the elements, were defining themselves more and more."[9]

In that third book, *Nik: Now I Know*, Julie obviously occupies more of the novel in terms of content than do the females in Chambers' earlier novels, but she also is allowed to share equal billing with Nik in terms of perception. In *Breaktime*, Helen is given agency in her sexual encounter with Ditto—she is certainly not just an object—but she is only one part of his experience while on his journey. His friend Morgan, his father, the two boys he commits the burglary with all play as important a role. In *Dance on My Grave*, the first draft of which was actually written before *Breaktime*, the Norwegian *au pair*, Kari, is the immediate cause of the breakup between Hal and Barry, but the focus of the book is decidedly on the male relationship, never on her. Julie, however, has a different role. For one thing, she is wanted by Nik but not for her body only, "not just for the sensation," as sex with Helen is wanted. *NIK: Now I Know* is not a novel of "pure sensation" as Chambers says *Breaktime* is. And Julie narrates, through her letters, at least as much of the novel as does Nik; her perception is equally important.

Perhaps it would be more accurate, however, to say not that this novel is more feminine but that it is less masculine. Julie makes the indisputable point that it makes as much sense to refer to God as "she" as it does to say "he." Julie herself is described as hermaphroditic, combining elements of both sexes, in the same way God is: When Nik first sees her at the peace rally, he says that she is wearing jeans that have been worn by a male "or else she was hermaphrodite" (*NIK*, 57). However, she is "not butch," just "tough-minded" (*NIK*, 84). Julie is also a follower of Dame Julian of Norwich, a fourteenth-century religious mystic who says in *Revelations of Divine Love*, "Jesus Christ, who sets good against evil, is our real Mother," and she explains why God's work can be described as "motherhood" (*NIK*, 131). Nik even comes to the conclusion that if Christ returned to earth today, it would be as a woman, reasoning thus:

   i. The universe is a binary system:
      Black holes/White holes;
      In/out;
      Male/female; etc.
   Last time God appeared as male;
      Next time as female. The system demands it.
   ii. The time of the domineering male is over;
       the time of the female has come.
   iii. Now the fish is returning to water. (*NIK*, 300–1)

Nik is explaining the world in terms of the ancient Chinese understanding represented in the symbol of yin yang. Everything in the universe can be divided into two opposing principles, but the dominance of one principle over another is only temporary. Every force (i.e., male/female) contains its opposite within it, and it is the action of these opposites that causes everything in the universe to happen. Clearly there is a shift beginning in *NIK: Now I Know*; it reaches its logical conclusion in Chambers' sixth novel in the "Dance Sequence," *This Is All: The Pillow Book of Cordelia Kenn*, which is narrated totally by a female.

TOM: MALE POINT OF VIEW AS IRONY

The third thread in the book concerns Tom, a police detective assigned to investigate the bizarre occurrence of a mysterious crucifixion. An early-morning jogger has seen someone hanging in a junkyard from some iron fashioned in the shape of a cross but dangling from a crane, not planted in the ground as was the case in ancient times. By the time he gets the police, the hanged one has disappeared. All he can say is that the person appeared to be a teenage boy, was wearing only navy-blue Y-front underpants, and was sweating and grinning. Tom is a young policeman, only nineteen, eager to prove himself when his superintendent assigns him to the case, "a kid to catch a kid," the sergeant says. He is described as keen and ambitious: "Naturally suspicious, he trusts nobody, not even his granny, possesses a certain dangerous charm, and is said to be at his best in tight corners" (*NIK*, 2). Tom is the dime-novel stereotype of the hard-boiled detective.

But then that's the point. The third thread, the story of the investigation, is written in the style of Mickey Spillane or Raymond Chandler and all those formulaic detective novels. Tom is desperate to prove himself, and he is smart enough to follow in the footsteps of those who have successfully come before him. He therefore asks around among the "lowlife," the petty criminals he can intimidate with his position: "What he needed was to know the chat. That was what all the Criminal Investigation Department bods started with. Straight on the blower to their snouts, thus saving themselves time and legwork. . . . At this present time of day there was only one place where the juvenile scum would be. Though eleven thirty was early for the best mouths. They'd still be festering in their pits, giving themselves hand jobs over page three [where one of the British tabloids always puts soft-porn pictures of nearly nude pin-ups] while waiting for their mums to nag them downstairs for midday fish and chips. But you never knew your luck" (*NIK*, 88–89). Tom is in fact in luck to find an old school acquaintance in the local pool hall, one he can bully into helping him out. He tells Sharkey, falsely, that the police superintendent actually thinks he did it: "Somebody has to know something. Shouldn't be too hard for you to give us a pointer that I can pass on to my guv. The culprit or culprits get collared and you get left alone. I get in good with the super, and that'll do me for now" (*NIK*, 104–5). Not only is Tom a stereotype but the style is a parody of the detective genre.

The reader learns as the investigation unfolds that Tom is not only unscrupulous but lascivious. The person Sharkey turns up as a possible lead is a teenage girl with a "fetching bum," Tom thinks. He also thinks that she might be useful for purposes other than his investigation: "Cop the braless knockers poking the cling-film vest. Here was evidence he'd like to get his grabbers on. No question: On a hot evening like this a forensic frig would nicely fit the bill. . . . The only thing she was good for was banged up in the slammer between her legs. As investigating officer he had a right of entry" (*NIK*, 254). When she suggests that they drive to a nearby park to talk, Tom is sure she means sex and acts, gropingly, on his desires. When she adroitly sidesteps his advances, he threatens her.

Tom's sexist attitude to women is pointed up by Nik's attitude to Julie and to Michelle, the girl Tom gracelessly gropes. He is Nik's foil, or doppelganger. Nik thoughtfully understands Julie's careful explanation why sex with him is out of the question for her. He even says that instead of Julie's turning him down, she has offered him something better, her loving friendship. And when he encounters Michelle shortly before Tom does, although she makes it clear that she would welcome his advances, he enjoys just talking to her, hearing what she has to say. The male point of view is valid only if combined with the female point of view.

PRACTICING THE CRUCIFIXION

Michelle knows about the crucifixion because Nik has asked her to help him do it, to himself. She refuses, of course, thinking that he is either feverish or still suffering from the bomb blast, but Nik is actually suffering from Julie's taped explanation of why what he wants, a man/woman love that includes sex, can't ever happen. She concludes her tape to him: "The love you've been wanting from me—the love that comes from the desire to be one—I've already given elsewhere, Nik. What I need is a friend who loves me as a friend, if I am to live up to that other love" (*NIK*, 266). Julie has had time to think in her hospital bed, and now she knows what relationship she wants with Nik, which is different from the oneness she wants with God. Julie's taped letters to Nik have been the process by which *she now knows* what she didn't before. Nik's notebook has been his process, his struggle to find the right words and to understand—Julie, belief, himself. He says early on that "finding the right words, putting them in their best order, is taking ages" but that "writing—doing the writing—also soothes me" (*NIK*, 162). And at various points in his writing he says *now I know*. As in *Breaktime* and *Dance on My Grave*, writing the story has been a means to understanding.

However, there comes a time when he can't write. He has just heard Julie's tape, and, as in the hospital with her for the last time, he is wracked with sobs. Words won't come, only tears. It's not just Julie's tape, though, that makes him crucify himself. He says that the real reason was hidden from even himself at the time, but immediately following is one of the "stockshots," with a quotation from Chekhov's *The Seagull*: "Now I know. . . . What matters most is knowing how to endure. Know how to bear your cross and have faith. I have faith and it doesn't hurt so much anymore" (*NIK*, 276). All along Nik has needed to know what faith is. Everyone he has talked to has told him that faith doesn't just happen; you have to *live* your faith. And so he reasons "as I am my own specimen, my own laboratory, and my own experiment . . . who else for the cross but me?" He, therefore, performs what he calls "a practice version" of the crucifixion, without nails or thorns or spears in the rib cage—he's not "a suicidal sadomasochist," he says (*NIK*, 275). In a clever bit of irony, Nik, whose middle name is Christopher, was chosen by the director of the film to play Jesus, and so it is in fact Jesus Christ who is crucified. The whole crucifixion story is given a modern twist: Nik has "disciples" (the Nikelodeons), the detective Tom is Doubting Thomas ("naturally suspicious, he trusts nobody"), and Michelle is the "loose woman" Mary Magdalene (good-hearted but sexually promiscuous).

After this "experiment," Nik can write again. That experience was, like Julie feels all the time, "being wholly myself and yet also more than myself, a part of something inevitable and beyond that moment" (*NIK*, 280). It gave him a clue, he says, "for cracking the code of the indecipherable" (*NIK*, 292). We see in Chambers' comments about another young seeker after self-knowledge and understanding, Anne Frank, how much he admires the tireless pursuit of answers to questions about life and one's place in it: "She studied life, using herself as her specimen, and found universal truths in herself. . . . Anne's Diary is a record of the human journey to self-consciousness."[10] She, like Nik, uses writing as a way to discover these truths.

IN THE BEGINNING WAS THE WORD

Despite the fact that Nik and Julie start from very different places—their contrast creates much of the tension in the novel—they conclude much the same thing. The last we hear from Julie, she "knows now" what she has to discover more about: "How to give my whole attention. What to give it to. What to do with it. . . . What I'm asking is: How do I remain myself, truly and without being crushed or diminished, while being one of the many, no more special and no more privileged, no more *noticeable*, and yet be wholly of God? . . . That's the question I have to give my whole attention to" (*NIK*, 298). She wants to do what the monks do in a monastery like the one that Chambers was a part of starting, not cutting herself off from people, living in purpose-built houses, or wearing special clothes, but "hidden among ordinary people in an ordinary everyday place" while she does "ordinary everyday work." For as Julie says, "Ordinary people must find God among themselves or they won't find her at all" (*NIK*, 298).

Nik also "knows now" what he says in his final letter to the film group. In order to make a film about Christ returning to the world today, they should "Sack the Director": "His kind of God doesn't exist anymore. You don't need him. Do it yourselves. Together. When you can, Christ has returned" (*NIK*, 301). The final word from both Julie and Nik is that God is not a being, nor is Christ, but us. Chambers uses a sun metaphor to try to convey this idea: As flecks of sunlight don't go looking for the sun because they are the sun, "in themselves and all together," people don't need to go looking for God, because they are God, "in ourselves and all together." St. John's

Gospel, a favorite of Chambers, Julie, and Nik, quoted by all of them, is key to the struggle for self-discovery that is *NIK: Now I Know*. "In the beginning was the word and the word was with God, and the word was God. . . . In him was life; and the life was the light of men." Only by words, and story, can we find who we are.

Chambers uses a variety of storying techniques in this novel. As in *Breaktime* and *Dance on My Grave*, the characters themselves share Chambers' interest in form and seek ways to best use words for their purpose. Since Nik's group is making a film, for example, he writes his story as if it is a film script, complete with "stockshots" and "intercuts." Instead of these stockshots being previously-shot footage of commonplace scenes—for a war movie, say, planes flying and infantrymen fighting, Nazis marching—they are more like voiceovers consisting of quotations from a variety of sources, which the "narrator" lists in an appendix: James Joyce's *Ulysses*, Shakespeare's *A Midsummer Night's Dream*, John Fowles' *The French Lieutenant's Woman*, Carl Jung, Simone Weil, the Bible, and others. A student essay printed on Chambers' website recognizes that these stockshots may at first appear random, but, in the manner of incidental music in a film or the way scenes are cut and juxtaposed, they actually can summarize a whole scene and help join one scene to another. They call the reader's attention to an idea, an important thought another writer has had. Readers then must make the connection—what does this thought have to do with that action?

For example, when Julie invites Nik to go with her to Norwich to visit the place where the religious visionary Dame Julian lived, Nik answers her, typically but slightly flippantly, with an elaborate acceptance that plays with numbers to get "the mystic trinity: three-in-one!" and plays with words revolving around "Thursday," the Norse mythological God Thor's day. Immediately after this letter to Julie accepting her invitation comes one of the "stockshots": "*There is only one definition of God: the freedom that allows other freedoms to exist*," a quotation that the appendix lists as from John Fowles' *The French Lieutenant's Woman* (*NIK*, 136). This quotation does three things. It comments on Nik's long rumination on old gods and the mystical belief in numbers. It also connects what came before—the information about numbers and about Thor—with what comes after—Nik's discovery that Maundy Thursday comes from Jesus' saying to his disciples on the day before he died, "A new commandment I give unto you," that they must love one another. And this stockshot also helps sum up the theme of the novel. The old gods, with their three heads and ten commandments, don't apply anymore. Now there is only one god—us—and one commandment: to love one another.

A similar effect is achieved by "intercuts." For example, as Nik describes to Julie his experience on a Swedish lake when he was young, in answer to her question whether he has ever experienced anything that made him wonder—even just for a minute—if there was "more to all this . . . than some sort of meaningless accident with meaningless ingredients inside the meaningless stewpot of a meaningless universe," he includes filming directions: "The Swedish lake in long shot, as before. Hold the scene: the dying sun's rays glancing on hilltops, the hut in dusktime shadow with the white ribbon of smoke rising, the little boat utterly still on the water. Five seconds. Then pull a steady, unhurried, soft-focus zoom towards the boat and its occupant" (*NIK*, 106). These and other techniques—for example, Nik's references to the writing on his word processor's green video display terminal or the audio transcripts of Julie's letters to Nik—serve to distance the reader from the action. We are never allowed to forget that we are "watching," or reading, an "artifact" or "fact of art" as Chambers calls it. We must *contemplate* and not just get caught up in the action. The techniques also force readers to participate in the process the protagonists go through in trying to make sense of the chaos of life. "Making the connections is what matters" (*NIK*, ii).

Chambers admits that it's language that interests him, that for him "In the beginning was the Word": "[W]e are all composed of the language we speak and think."

Story, he says, is "the form in which we use language to create and recreate ourselves—our ideas about who we are, where we have come from, what we might be. Language is the god who makes us" (*SAAAS*, 52). However, language, when we come to speak or write about spiritual matters, has certain limitations. How, for example, can meditation be represented by words, when by its very definition words must be bypassed? Nik struggles to convey his experience of meditative Silence in the monastery that he goes to in order to recover, mentally, from the bomb blast, and he comes up with "word clusters." When Nik meditates, words come to him in clusters, which make an object, something three-dimensional, and mobile. When he tries to write a cluster down, his retreat director calls it a poem. Although Nik objects that he can't write poetry, his cluster certainly can't be read like prose; it looks more like a crossword puzzle where words must be read down as well as across. That explanation, however, isn't entirely accurate because Nik says that a cluster is three-dimensional, a little like a mobile sculpture, or a hologram. Since this mobile is impossible to reproduce on the printed page, Nik must give directions for reading the cluster, for imagining its movement. A critic writing on recent experiments with form by young adult authors points out that in describing this cluster Chambers by extension is asking readers to envision, with their imaginations, both it and "its literary possibilities."[11] Readers must collaborate with Chambers' protagonists in their struggle with language; they must "make the connections."

POETRY AND RELIGION—YIN AND YANG

Chambers is convinced that the only way one can talk about spirituality is with poetry, which, the reader sees, is the conclusion Nik comes to at the end. Yet, Chambers notes, the last four pages of *NIK: Now I Know* are often overlooked, even though they are "the important bit." In those pages Nik has written four poems for Julie. He has not "converted." He has not come to believe what she believes. But he has come to understand that rational, scientific inquiry can't work. That's what Chambers believes to be true: "The only way you can actually discuss spiritual matters—talk about them—is in poetic language, in poetry, in literary forms, which is why all religions have a literary base. They are all a collection of stories, actually. Scientific investigations of spirituality always fail because you can't find it in the brain. That's what Nik says by the end of the book, that's what he's doing, and I believe that to be true."[12] Nik punctuates his text by the word "selah," a Hebrew word used in the Bible at the end of passages in Psalms. Nik's story becomes his bible.

Aidan Chambers recalls in almost religious terms the importance Jim Osborn, the teacher whom he credits with changing his life, placed on a literary education. Osborn, Chambers says, believed passionately that the heart of all education, and the heart of all culture, must be literature: "As a scientist, as an historian, anything, literature has to be the basis of your education, otherwise you'll go wrong. Jim believed that passionately, and he communicated that passion. . . . I still believe that to be true. I still believe the heart of any education has to be story." He considers himself "that now very disparaged person" who believes that art is currently a religion—that the telling of stories is the current form of secular religion. One of the reasons he left the monastery, he says, is that he found he couldn't subscribe to the central tenets of the church as historically and literally true, and even though many in the church were already arguing that these tenets could be taken metaphorically, not literally, he felt that he had become a part of the church for the wrong reasons. The finest English language, the theater, the silence and meditative thinking, and the ritual of life all appealed to a fundamental part of him, he says, but he could have those in a life dedicated to a cause he believed in—writing.[13]

The four poems that conclude *Nik: Now I Know* contain many versions of "the kiss of two cones," spirals, the symbol of yin and yang—oppositions joined, "end without end," which are the last words of the novel. For as Nik says, "but for the poet living in ourselves we wouldn't learn anything"—about faith, about belief, about ourselves (*NIK*, 306). Thus, Nik's book, arising out of his experiences, becomes a *sui generis* holy book, a personal bible that leads him to the truth about himself. As Chambers says, "All religions have a literary base. They're all a collection of stories. . . . Most of the principal ones have a holy book, based on one person. . . . There isn't one holy book [laughs] because everybody by now is putting together their own holy book."[14] This may explain why so much of Chambers' *oeuvre* is about people writing books. We all are capable of writing The Gospel According to Me.

NOTES

1. Chambers, personal interview.
2. Chambers, personal interview.
3. Chambers, personal interview.
4. Chambers, personal interview.
5. Chambers, personal interview.
6. Aidan Chambers, *NIK: Now I Know* (New York: Harper, 1987), ii. Hereafter cited in the text as *NIK*.
7. Colin Greenland, "Review of *Now I Know*," *Times Literary Supplement* (3 April 1987). Quoted on Chambers' website.
8. Chambers, personal interview.

9. Chambers, personal interview.
10. Chambers, personal website. Retrieved from www.aidanchambers.co.uk/journalism/journalism3.htm. First given as his Hans Christian Andersen Award acceptance speech.
11. Lauren Adams, "Disorderly Fiction," *The Horn Book Magazine* 78.5 (Sep/Oct 2002), 2. Academic Search Premier. 28 January 2004. Keyword: Chambers, Aidan.
12. Chambers, personal interview.
13. Chambers, personal interview.
14. Chambers, personal interview.

Chapter 5

A Ghostly Fugue:
The Toll Bridge

By the time Aidan Chambers had finished the third novel in the "Dance Sequence," *NIK: Now I Know*, he knew there was a pattern emerging. In each of the novels, he says, he saw "a different kind of love story—that's the principle of each one."[1] What he didn't know, however, was out of which particle of what he calls "the anthology that is our inner world" would come the next novel. This anthology, for Chambers, is made up of a jumble of stories—things that have happened to him but also stories that come to him "out of the blue," from "fantasies, day-dreams, imaginings of different kinds."[2] Wherever the story comes from, however, it has its basis in real life. His stories always use real places as settings, and they always come out of an event in everyday life.

The story that was to become *The Toll Bridge* originated in one of these "imaginings," while he was still writing *NIK: Now I Know* in 1985. He remembers its beginnings vividly: "Once a week I was traveling between my home and Oxford, where I was teaching a course. I had to cross the Swinford toll bridge, where the same man stood in the middle of the road every day taking the money from the passing cars. He was always dressed, rain or shine, in the same dirty old macintosh, woolen hat, woolen mittens, weary gray flannel trousers tucked into thick grey socks, and worn-out old boots. He said nothing as he took the money, but I noticed that his Adam's apple moved up and down each time." When Chambers remarked on this to a friend of his, he was given a copy of the local history society's booklet celebrating the 200th anniversary of the bridge in 1965, and in it was a photograph of the toll keeper at that time, "a young man in a clean-looking macintosh and big boots." Chambers continues, "He was, of course, the same man as the one I had seen, so for the whole of his life he must have done nothing but take money from passing cars. The movement of his Adam's apple was, I realised, the vestigial remains of his saying 'Thank you. Thank you' each time. Why, I wondered, would a young man take such a dreary job and do it for the rest of his working life? I began to speculate, and the story that became *The Toll Bridge* emerged from my imaginings."[3] Chambers' speculations led him to combine that kernel of a story with a love story of a kind previous novels in the "Dance Sequence" had touched on but hadn't explored fully, what Chambers says was called "bosom friendship" in his generation, the kind of friendship that he had experienced with Marion when they were children in Chester-le-Street.

Piers, seventeen and clinically depressed, takes a job as toll collector at a small private bridge on an estate in the south of England in order to get away from a life where he feels smothered by parents, girlfriend, and school. Into his life come the estate manager's daughter, who re-christens him Jan, after Janus, the mythological god of bridges, and a mysterious drifter to whom both are attracted but about whom they know nothing. Jan at first wants to be rid of this intruder, Adam, because he's intensely jealous, but he lets him stay and help renovate the toll-keeper's cottage, for reasons he doesn't understand himself. The complicated relationships among this triangle drive the story, which is about the mysteries of attraction and of personality, about lost souls and hidden lives. Above all, who is Adam?

If *Breaktime* is about physical sensation, *Dance on My Grave* about emotional obsession, and *NIK: Now I Know* about spiritual belief (a schema Chambers says he articulated at his publisher's request—"not untrue, just crude"[4]), then *The Toll Bridge* is about psychological development. "The power of the peer group is much greater than it used to be," explains Chambers, "and there is such a commercial nature about what you wear, what you listen to, that a literature that speaks about the hidden inner person is more important than it has ever been."[5] *The Toll Bridge* is about discovering that hidden inner person and, in the process, discovering oneself.

WHAT'S IN A NAME

Names are important in all of Chambers' works, as we have seen, but they take on a special significance in this one. All of the main characters have two names, their birth name and one given by another character in the book. Piers at first resists the name "Jan," given to him by Katherine, the daughter of the manager of the estate on which he has come to work. Although Piers is very private and keeps to himself when he first arrives, very depressed and "looking like a ghost," he allows himself to accept some help from this "high-energy girl" sent by her father to make sure Piers stays, for he was the only applicant for the job.[6] Janus, the pre-Roman god of bridges but also of doors and passages and archways, has two faces looking in opposite directions. Katherine says to Piers shortly after he arrives, "You keep the bridge and you're also two-faced, so I'll call you Jan, son of Janus" (*Toll*, 36). She argues that he is two-faced because he is keeping his girlfriend back home "on a string" while he is flirting outrageously with her and because he is clearly jealous of the drifter Adam—who has just appeared seemingly out of the blue—but won't admit it. When he protests that Jan is a girl's name, he is told that it is both, signaling his ambivalent sexuality. Jan is an appropriate name because, as Katherine says, he "looks both ways at once and can't make up his mind which way to go because he doesn't know whether he's coming or going" (*Toll*, 37). That is Jan's situation.

Jan admits that he's confused. In fact, the reason he has taken the toll-keeper's job far from his home is that he's tired of pretending to be what everyone else wants, the responsible son, lover, and student. He is an only child of parents who lost an earlier baby to crib death and now desperately cling to him, the boyfriend of a suffocating girl almost blackmailing him with memories of their past sex life, and good student accelerated one year by teachers sure that anything other than more school is a waste. A depressed and exhausted Jan now wants to escape, wants time to find out, as he tells his girlfriend back home, "what I really *truly* am. Who I am, I mean." He doesn't want to be responsible for anyone else and doesn't like "all this talk about love": "What people call love is only things they want from someone else. Like a good screw or a nice time together or even just someone to keep them from feeling lonely" (*Toll*, 24–25). All he knows is that he doesn't want the responsibilities that come with being an adult—"some endless job," a family, a mortgage, and a house to keep up—but he also doesn't want "to go on being a schoolkid either." "Stuck in limboland," Katherine says (*Toll*, 39).

Katherine becomes "Tess," re-christened by Jan ostensibly because she brings him groceries from the supermarket Tesco's. Although its connotations are never mentioned, the name Tess, like the name Helen in *Breaktime*, is especially appropriate because it suggests certain qualities associated with a literary namesake. The protagonist of Thomas Hardy's *Tess of the d'Urbervilles* is caught between two men, one ethereal and intellectual, like Jan, and the other dark, dangerous, and sexually magnetic, like Adam. She becomes an unwilling center of this triangle, desired by both. However, the high-energy girl in *The Toll Bridge* is an ironic Tess, or at least a modern version; rather than a victim of sex, like Hardy's character, this Tess is an empowered woman, one who, like Helen in *Breaktime*, initiates and enjoys sex. She is as much the seducer as the seduced. Though momentarily worried, sensibly, that a sexual encounter will result in pregnancy or disease, she escapes consequences, unlike her nineteenth-century precursor, Tess of the d'Urbervilles.

Her sexual partner, like the seducer of the earlier Tess, is the dark and dangerous one. Adam appears "like a ghost" at Jan's bedside, forcing the lock on the tollhouse because he is looking for a place to sleep and thinks it is abandoned. At least Jan thinks that's his name, for when he says "I don't know you from Adam," the intruder says "Right first time." As he stands before Jan shedding his wet clothes, because he has fallen in the river, his "well-endowed" body—the kind, Jan says, "boys in shower rooms honor with surreptitious glances"—and his black, wet hair are the only things known about him, then or later (*Toll*, 4–5). Everything else is a mystery. The story of his past changes every time he tells it. He appears and disappears without explanation, ghostlike. But he is enormously attractive, and sexy; neither Jan nor Tess wants to let him go.

Adam is not his birth name, as we learn at the end, but it suggests much about what he is and what he represents. As the first man, the biblical Adam is a blank slate, a *tabula rasa* with no past. He is formed from the dust of the earth. He is also innocent, with no knowledge, like a child. When he is tempted by Eve to eat the apple, however, he tastes of the knowledge of good and evil. In *The Toll Bridge*, Adam also has no past, because he has forgotten it. He makes it up as he goes along. The reader learns only at the end, along with Jan and Tess, that Adam is really Aston, a boy with a very guilty past. Adam/Aston is in effect two people. He has a condition known to psychiatrists as the Fugue state.

His doctor describes Adam as "a happy-go-lucky uninhibited guilt-free sexy young man" (*Toll*, 264). Aston, on the other hand, has headaches and nightmares, is tormented by his past to the point of suicidal wishes. Adam has uninhibited, "mindlost" sex with Tess, who, we learn, was "lusty" and "insatiable" and "didn't care," who had grabbed the chance to lead this Adam into sexual experience (*Toll*, 155). Aston is a child who plays all day in a tree house and whose best friend is Robinson Crusoe. When Jan suggests that Adam has somehow *regressed* from a seventeen-year-old to an eleven-year-old, the doctor says life isn't that simple, not "a linear journey, birth point A to death point Z"; it is rather a multiplicity of actualities and potentialities. He elaborates: "One of the many things the so-called mentally ill have taught me is that we so-called healthy people are not very good at exploring our possible selves. Perhaps because we feel reasonably happy with the selves we are living. But perhaps we are the most imprisoned of all because of that. Whereas the mentally ill, being uncomfortable with their actual selves, sometimes explore their potentialities and find selves they like better and try them out" (*Toll*, 265). The Adam that is Everyman has shown that, as Chambers has suggested in his other novels, personality is not one thing; what we think of as our *self* is actually *selves*.

ADAM AS SECRET SHARER

Although we are *selves* and not one self, the various aspects of personality need to be integrated if we are not to enter the Fugue state (when a person goes on the run, forgets a previous life, and invents a new one), become autistic, try to commit suicide, or become self-destructive or anti-social in any way. These selves need to be recognized and acknowledged, as the doctor suggests the "mentally ill" are good at doing, but ultimately they need to be integrated. Adam symbolically helps Jan to integrate, to face life and make decisions rather than run away, as Tess says Jan is doing at the toll bridge. Adam effects this in his role as *doppelganger* or secret sharer.

Adam and Jan's situation parallels that of Joseph Conrad's secret sharer and ship's captain, as many of Chambers' characters do. (See chapter two for a fuller explanation of Conrad's story.) Adam appears, "like a ghost," wet and naked in Jan's room. Against all reason, Jan finds himself taking him in: "Given the obvious idiocy of taking in, like a feral dog in the middle of the night, someone I know nothing about, except he is called Adam, has an enviable cock, and has just been careless enough to fall into the river, my second surprise of the night comes when I hear myself say, 'Sure. Expect we can fix something up'" (*Toll*, 5). Jan thinks to himself that he's got to get rid of this intruder as soon as he can, but he keeps letting him stay on, giving him clothes to wear and food to eat. Like Conrad's captain, Jan is nervous at being on his own for the first time in his life, and like the captain he takes in the wet, naked "secret sharer." He, like the captain, is constantly taken aback when his ghostly visitor vanishes "in a puff of smoke" when other people come near.

Also like the two characters in Conrad's story, Chambers' characters are on the surface opposites. Adam is everything Jan is not. As Adam rows a dinghy on the river that flows under the toll bridge, Jan is consumed with jealousy as he watches his "steady effortless strokes": "His body has an animal perfection in its proportions, the neat way all its parts fit together, the easy relaxed way it moves, beautiful to watch, very sexy" (*Toll*, 32). Jan, on the other hand, rows back home feeling "awkward," "like an alien." He has a good memory for literary quotations, is what teachers call "clever," and is liked by Tess for his mind. Reading, to him, is an essential part of his life. Adam has no memory at all. He left school early and never reads. He is all body, whereas Jan is all brain. That dichotomy is brought home as Tess and Adam have sex while Jan, hidden from them, watches—and watches himself watching. He is amazed to find that instead of jealousy or rage or even lust, he feels a calming satisfaction, like "watching a close friend doing something he's good at and doing it very well. You might wish you could do it well too while knowing that you couldn't" (*Toll*, 128). Jan is having his sex, as D. H. Lawrence would say, "in the head." These two are as different as Dr. Jekyll is from Mr. Hyde.

When Adam is seriously injured, Jan must take care of him. He still wonders why but knows now that it is inevitable. The descriptions emphasize their coming together, their oneness. Jan tries to move him, "lifted him into a sitting position, his head lolling against my shoulder, his cheek pressing against my cheek, the oily wetness of cold blood lubricating our skins" (*Toll*, 169). Jan begins to realize then how much he has changed, *grown*, in the time he has been at the toll bridge. At first it is signaled by small things. He is proud of himself, for example, for not fainting at the mere thought of tending Adam's wounds, as he would have done just months before. Later, he truly accepts the name Jan, deciding to never again call himself Piers, that day becoming "his chosen birthday" (*Toll*, 212). But he still doesn't want to let Adam go: "To let him go, to send him away, would be a loss to himself and a dereliction" (*Toll*, 210). As Jan tries to explain to Tess why it is so important that Adam stay at the toll house and be protected from well-meaning but interfering adults, he *feels* intuitively rather than understands intellectually: "I keep thinking. . . . It's as if he were me. No, not me. I mean—the other me. Christ; I don't know! It's too hard to explain" (*Toll*, 217). Like Conrad's captain and secret sharer, Jan feels an inexplicable but powerful attraction to this secret being. And in a cross between Joseph Conrad and D. H. Lawrence, the two males in Chambers' story finally share the ultimate closeness—the same bed. It is not a sexual sharing, but a physicality, a "satisfaction of the body" where Jan gets warmth from Adam as much as Adam gets warmth from Jan. At that moment Jan is at peace, with no depression and no headaches, for the first time since he came to the toll bridge. And at that moment, Jan understands, intuitively, the oppositions that make up his life. "I am Janus, he thought, guarding the bridge, biding my time. Dually watchful. Of the other, of myself. Of outer, of inner. Of my him, of my her. Constant ambivalence, happy ambiguity" (*Toll*, 225).

SHIFT TO THE FEMALE

One of those oppositions that Jan hints at is his new-found empathy with women. He decides to apologize to his girlfriend back home for the awful way he has treated her, and he becomes the comforter, the carer for Tess rather than being the comforted and the cared for as he has been until then. Tess feels his new decisiveness: "He's changed, grown. More certain of himself. How much I like him" (*Toll*, 234–35). Jan even recognizes the built-in sexism in the language and starts to change the way he writes. He calls what Tess does "work[wo]manship" (*Toll*, 216). Tess breaks into Jan's narrative more and more, telling parts of the story from her point of view, until at the end they agree to narrate together, without, Tess insists, all of Jan's "male-order stuff like those titles and numbered sections and everything all very ordered and in charge, and literary crossword puzzles and quoting from poets nobody reads and stuff like that" (*Toll*, 194). The first part of the narrative had been told by Jan with a complicated numbering system, with divisions and subdivisions.

Jan's girlfriend from home, Gill, also plays a role in this story and in this shift to the female, so that by the end there is a quartet, rather than a trio of two boys and a girl, as there has been in all of Chambers' previous novels. We hear Gill's voice through her letters to Jan at the beginning, increasingly desperate to get some kind of response from Jan/Piers. Tess keeps telling Jan how unfair he is being to Gill by refusing to let her come see him but also refusing to end their relationship, so through her words we are allowed to see things from Gill's point of view. It is a measure of Jan's maturity at the end that he does indeed begin to see things through her eyes: "He suddenly saw all the past few months from her vantage, saw how he and everything at the house must have looked to her. He could not believe that he had been so unthinking, so unfeeling, so unknowing" (*Toll*, 230). Tess knew long before Jan did that he needed to open himself to the female point of view.

Chambers says that he feels a similar shift going on in himself, as discussed in the previous chapter about *NIK: Now I Know*. He describes his earlier writing as very "male-centred." The world, and the word, was "he." However, the pattern of the novels in the "Dance Sequence" describes a gradual shift, so by the last one, *This Is All: The Pillow Book of Cordelia Kenn*, not only is the subject a girl, but she is also the narrator. Chambers says he has felt a similar shift go on in himself, not sexually, of course, but in perception, "how you understand things, how you look at the world."[7] This is one way in which the experience of writing the novels has changed him, in the same way that his protagonists are changed by the very process of writing their experience. All of his novels validate writing as discovery, especially discovery of self, as does his own writing experience. One of Chambers' favorite quotations is by W. H. Auden: "How do I know what I think until I see what I say?"

THE FORM OF THE FUGUE

Writing is essential to Jan, as it is to Chambers, and it is also discovery. Tess lets us know that Jan is "only ever really truly happy when he's writing: It's the only time when he's in focus—when he's doing what he says he lives for" (*Toll*, 150). Jan doesn't know, however, at least not at first, that he is writing for his own self-discovery. Jan writes, in a kind of preface that only becomes entirely clear after reading the whole novel, "For Adam. Take this as a gift. The only gift I can give you that might, one day, mean anything to you"(*Toll*, 1). As in J. D. Salinger's *The Catcher in the Rye*, where the entire story is told by Holden Caulfield to his psychiatrist, the book that is *The Toll Bridge* is being told to another, to Adam. Not only told, though, but written. Jan argues in this "preface" that he is writing it so that Adam will be able to learn something from it about himself: "And what will you do? About yourself, I mean. That's the only important question. One reason why I'm writing this is to show you how you seemed to me, to us, how we thought of you" (*Toll*, 1). As becomes clear as the novel proceeds, however, Jan is writing it as much for himself as for Adam. More, really. As Tess also tells us, "Writing Adam's story has something to do with his hiddenness. I think it's a story about himself, maybe a declaration" (*Toll*, 151).

As Chambers himself comments, although the story seems to be told to Adam/Aston, it is really being told to Jan himself. Even those novels that seem to be addressed to a specific character, Chambers explains, are really addressed to the person who is writing the book, in order to understand him- or herself: "Not him-herself now—at the time of writing. Perhaps him-herself at a much later time. Or, to put it better, his-her 'other self,' a self that co-exists with his-her writing self."[8] The largest part of *The Toll Bridge*, then, is ostensibly written for Adam and consists of Jan's account of what happened during the few short weeks that Tess, Adam, and he spent together. This traditional narrative is broken in on—by italicized comments by Tess to Jan while he is writing, by letters from Jan's parents and girlfriend, by Jan's questionings about how he can best tell his story—so that the reader is constantly being made aware of the *writing* and not just of the story. At one point Jan even writes, ". . . and the tin bath that's used in a page or two" (*Toll*, 65). Joseph Conrad uses similar techniques in *Heart of Darkness* to remind readers that the story is being told by a narrator, Marlow, and to remind us that the story is as much about Marlow as about his dark *doppelganger*, Kurtz. In this way, *The Toll Bridge* is very much a part of the metafictional quality of all the novels in the "Dance Sequence."

The narrative structure of the novel is different from those of the others, however. It is individual, as it must be, in order to solve different narrative problems. At first it is unified by having a predominately one first-person voice. (The letters from Jan's parents and girlfriend are clearly inserted by Jan because he wants his narrative to be a complete account of the weeks he is writing about and because during those weeks he shows those letters to Tess for her input.) The narrative is interrupted, however, by Tess, whose words are at first in italics to indicate that she is speaking. She essentially corrects Jan's narrative: *"What you didn't know at the time . . . "* or *"I know you've got to tell this story the way you remember it, but this last scene just isn't right"* (*Toll*, 16; 66). Soon she writes whole sections, without the italics: "Because he wasn't there, Jan doesn't know what happened next, so I'll tell it . . . " (*Toll*, 150). Almost the last sixty pages of the novel are told by both of them, for as Tess reasons to Jan, *"then we can get in everything we both knew"* (*Toll*, 193). They become a third-person narrator, referring to themselves as "Tess" and "Jan" instead of "I" as they had done in their individual sections. This gradual shift, as well as indicating a male to female movement in the overall "Dance Sequence," shows how important Tess has become to Jan—how important they are to each other. Form mirrors content.

The last few pages are again written by Jan. One reason is that he is the only one who visits Aston-Adam, as Jan now calls him, in the psychiatric prison, and so only he knows what happens there. The reason Chambers has him be the only one, however, is because only he "needs to," as the doctor says (*Toll*, 268). Jan visits and Jan writes for the same reason: to quiet his conscience, he says, about leaving Adam (*Toll*, 1). Tess calls Jan's writing "a declaration" and "a confession" (*Toll*, 151; 109). Adam's doctor knows that he visits and he writes because, as he tells Jan, "You've got a story to tell. Everybody has" (*Toll*, 268). That story isn't just about Adam, though. As Tess realizes, that story is really about Jan.

THE LOVE OF A FRIEND

As Jan learns about himself, he learns how much he has come to need Tess. The reader discovers that the story is being written two years after the events that are being described, so the writers—Jan but also Tess—have had two years' perspective. What they have come to understand is their relationship to each other. Jan describes it as "the first true friendship of my life. My closest friendship still" (*Toll*, 16). He is less demonstrative than Tess is, but for that reason what little he says holds special weight. When he sees her having sex with Adam, he knows, accepts, that "Tess was not, would not be, for me nor me for her" (*Toll*, 128). That is, they would not be sexual lovers. But that is only the beginning of the understanding of what they *would* be, not the end. Each realizes this after a particularly long and angry separation:

> [A]s soon as he saw Tess, all Jan's weariness and the anger he felt for what she had done during the last three days evaporated. The very sight of her was enough to revive his spirits.
>
> Stopped in her tracks by the sight of Jan, Tess suddenly felt confused, all her determination draining away, surprised by the strength of her feelings at seeing him again, as if they had been parted for years.
>
> They gazed at each other for a long moment, neither saying anything, both aware of the moment's significance, knowing beyond a doubt for the first time that each was irreplaceable to the other no matter what. . . . (*Toll*, 195)

Sexual love is only one kind of love. *The Toll Bridge*, like *NIK: Now I Know*, demonstrates that love between friends is just as strong and just as true.

Tess is surprised, like Jan is, to discover this truth. She has never before met someone who makes her think and discuss like Jan does, and so says with some amazement, "What I like most about you is your mind" (*Toll*, 45). Her revelation goes even further: "We talk about *everything*, which is another reason I like him so much (love him, I suppose). . ." (*Toll*, 151). Her understanding of love is quite different from what Jan says most people mean by it, which is selfish, almost cannibalistic. When he first comes to the toll bridge, before he comes to love Tess, he tells his girlfriend back home, angrily, "What people call love is only things they want from someone else. . . . Eating people is wrong" (*Toll*, 24–25). What Tess and Jan have is not understood by "most people." They sustain each other, and will for life. At the end, when a shaken Tess asks Jan "[D]o I matter that much?" Jan takes a deep breath, considers, and answers, "Nobody more" (*Toll*, 237).

There is another kind of love examined here—also a love between friends but between friends of the same sex. In this regard, *The Toll Bridge* resembles another D. H. Lawrence novel, *Women in Love*. There is also a quartet of two men and two women in that novel, and the two men have a special bond. Lawrence's Rupert is most like Jan, a thinker and a reader. Gerald is most like Adam, both having an impulsive, violent side; both have inadvertently caused a death; in both there is something missing, inside. Gerald commits suicide; Adam tries. Two scenes in particular in *The Toll Bridge* sound a Laurentian echo.

In one scene, Adam tries to give Jan a silver chain, but when Jan rejects it the two end up wrestling: "I knock his hand away, sending the chain flying across the room. We struggle, saying nothing, wrestling, not half-hearted, not playful, but using all our strength, meaning it. A contest" (*Toll*, 91). A central scene in *Women in Love* is also a wrestling contest between the two men, there stripped of their clothes, naked in front of the fire. Much later, Jan tends a wounded and frightened Adam, trying to calm him first by hugging him tightly, then by lying with him, and finally by falling asleep with him. The next day Jan recognizes that he was as much calmed by their contact as Adam was: "Till last night he had never known the power of physicality. Not cock-pleasure, but satisfaction of the body. Flesh and bone on flesh and bone. And the gut-felt, beyond-thought need of it" (*Toll*, 25). Above all, D. H. Lawrence believed in a life based on the physical, on sensual physicality. The physical may include but goes beyond sex. Many of the arguments in *Women in Love* concern Rupert's insistence on a need for another sort of affection than his wife's affection. He wants *blutbruderschaft* (blood brotherhood) with Gerald. Chambers, too, suggests that "bosom friendship," whether between the same or different sexes, is as powerful as sexual love and that physicality is a powerful need, so powerful that Rupert feels it could have saved Gerald from suicide.

BOOKS AS HELPERS

Lawrence is not the only author Chambers knows and likes well enough to call on in his writing, as we have seen. Reading is so important to him and he has read so widely that books naturally form the foundation of his work. Chambers even says on his website that reading other favorite authors is an important part of writing his own novels, to help him with either narrative form or content. A truth "not usually admitted in public," Chambers says, is that "all writing is theft. You take from other writers what helps you, and recycle it into something of your own."[9] While he was writing each of his novels there were a few key books that he says he read almost obsessively. For *The Toll Bridge* it was Iris Murdoch, especially *The Good Apprentice* and *The Philosopher's Pupil*.[10] Murdoch is a complex novelist, trained in philosophy and intensely interested in ideas, just the kind of novelist Chambers most likes.

Some of the correspondences between these books are obvious. *The Good Apprentice* is an allegorical story, like most of Murdoch's work, of the battle between good and evil. One of the characters in that work believes he has killed his friend and suffers terrible remorse. In *The Toll Bridge*, Adam not only believes it but has been convicted of manslaughter. In *The Philosopher's Pupil* there is a character named Adam—a young boy—who is confused about his identity, in this case predominately his sexual identity. There is also a scene of two men embracing in bed, but the nature of this embrace is not clear. In many of Murdoch's characters it is impossible to rigidly categorize gender preferences—either for themselves or for sexual partners. Murdoch, like Chambers, shows interest throughout her work in the multiplicity of personality and the impossibility of placing humans in neat pigeon-holes according to a rigid binary system of gender and sexuality. As she states in "Against Dryness," human beings are "impenetrable, individual [and] indefinable."[11] The doctor in *The Toll Bridge* similarly says, "We are multiple beings" (*Toll*, 265).

Kafka is another writer very important to *The Toll Bridge*, especially his story "The Bridge." After Tess and Jan listen one evening to Adam tell about a scary dream in which he tries but can't cross a bridge, Jan reads them Kafka's surrealistic story, in which a man actually *is* a bridge. Adam appears to understand intuitively and says, "It's the stones, the stones in the rushing water" (*Toll*, 108). Looking back from the perspective of two years later, Tess says to Jan, "[I]t didn't seem to occur to us that Adam's dream was about a bridge and Kafka's story was about a bridge and that there we all were sitting by a bridge, and that bridges are always about connecting two separated things, about joining things together that can't meet otherwise, and about crossing from one side to the other. In either direction. That bridges are at borders and boundaries." She brings up another writer, Italo Calvino, who has since clarified Adam's comment for her: "We didn't understand yet that, yes, we are each individual stones, but that together we can make an arch" (*Toll*, 109). Kafka's story comes up later in *The Toll Bridge* as Jan tries to take care of Adam, hurt and with no memory. At that moment he says the story seems oddly appropriate to his life: "He and Adam and Tess:

each other's bridges, as Kafka's young man had become a bridge for someone else." But Jan doesn't know whether it tells what would be or what could be (*Toll*, 210). Jan crosses. He is scared, but he takes those steps to maturity that the reader has seen: tending Adam, apologizing to his girlfriend, supporting Tess in her lowest moment. As Jan writes, "So cross with care. But cross you must" (*Toll*, 230). Adam can't cross. He gets to the middle and tries to throw himself off. He is still stuck in his childhood anguish over his violent past.

Chambers makes allusions to many writers and many books, stories, and poems throughout *The Toll Bridge*. Besides Kafka, there are quotations from or references to Samuel Beckett, Shakespeare, Dylan Thomas, Gerard Manley Hopkins, D. H. Lawrence, *Robinson Crusoe*, *The Wind in the Willows*, and "Sleeping Beauty," among others. Chambers even quotes from his own novels, though he doesn't identify them (*Toll*, 177–78). In terms of overt plot this makes sense because Jan is a reader and a quoter. It characterizes him. Allusions serve a purpose other than making readers feel superior for recognizing them, however, as Tess comments at one point when Jan wants her to guess the source of a quotation. Allusions connect a work to the larger world of art and ideas. They expand a reader's response to a work by bringing in other works and making the reader make the connection. For example, when Jan thinks, twice, of Puck's line from *A Midsummer Night's Dream*, "What fools these mortals be," he is thinking of his own foolishness but also how he is a part of the larger pattern of human foolishness. In Shakespeare's play, the sprite Puck is amused at the entanglements humans get themselves into, but the humans are really being manipulated by the magical fairies, if they could only see. Therefore, when Jan asks himself, "Could these be mere accidents, unconnected coincidences?" (*Toll*, 211), the suggestion the whole book makes, aided by that quotation, is "No."

If there are more allusions in this novel than in Chambers' others, perhaps it is because making connections and seeing patterns are so important to the whole ethos of *The Toll Bridge*. After Jan quotes many writers on "heads" as he bandages Adam's unconscious one, he says, "What stupid things come into your mind at such times. Yet not stupid, if you think about it. Pertinent and true in unthought ways. Is anything that comes into your mind ever arbitrary, ever meaningless?" (*Toll*, 173). Jan comes to understand that everything is part of a larger pattern even if it is not clear to us at the time.

INTUITION AND SYMBOL

The understanding, however, is intuitive and not logical, as Jan has been up to this point in his life. He has trusted thoughts because he could be in charge of them, rather than feelings, which were in charge of him. As he realizes about himself, "So in all things Jan had come to prefer the life of the mind" (*Toll*, 211). Because of Adam, however, he has learned to trust intuition. When Adam first appears, Jan has a strong sense of déjà vu, which feels to him like a "revelation"; it has happened before so it is inevitable. He has felt *NIK*'s "kiss of two cones," where the past meets and merges with the present. As he plunges into something totally new with Adam, where he doesn't have experience to guide him, he turns to intuition, "his newly trusted guide" (*Toll*, 224).

Jan's process of moving from logical thought to intuition is very much like the experience Chambers describes going through himself. His teacher Jim Osborn was what Chambers calls "totally intellectual": "You weren't allowed to say 'I feel that . . . , ' which was his weak side. He was brought up in the English grammar school—rational, intellectual. Had no idea of intuition at all. All that had been rationalized out of him." When Chambers filled in a questionnaire for a California research group doing a psychological study of writers—"just for fun"—he got back an "astonishing" report: "This person is an intuitive thinker who has been turned into a rational intellectual. When I saw it I thought, that's exactly what happened." With *Breaktime*, he says he had to give himself up to the intuitive, which he had been denied since he was fifteen. As described in the first chapter, when he became stuck in his writing before he started *Breaktime*, he went with what was totally unintellectual, "because I didn't know what else to do." He credits his seven years in the monastery with helping him to recover his intuitive side: "Meditative prayer is not a rational, intellectual matter. In meditation you're not sitting there doing rational thinking; you are going somewhere else. . . . During that time I didn't know it, but I was recovering." Intuition, he says, produced *Breaktime*, and so "now I trust it totally." Only after he has followed his intuition in a book will he try to work out "why it's there, what it's doing," to become conscious of his aims and methods.[12]

Symbolism works similarly on two levels. A symbol functions in a story as something real, yet it also stands for an abstract idea. *The Toll*

Bridge makes use of many symbols, beginning with the title itself, which, like all of Chambers' titles, has more than one meaning. The bridge is a real bridge, based on the one in Oxfordshire. Jan and his friends row on the river it spans; Adam plays Pooh-sticks from it and swings like Tarzan over it. It allows for many of the happenings in the novel to take place. Bridges, however, are often used as symbol, have even entered the language as metaphor. We say that we need to "bridge the gap" or "build bridges between nations" or "cross that bridge when we come to it." We don't want to "burn our bridges." Kafka's story uses the bridge symbolically. Tess and Jan recognize its symbolic meaning when they say that the three friends are each other's bridges. Finally, "cross with care but cross we must." As Victor Watson notes in his introduction to the entry on Aidan Chambers in *Coming of Age in Children's Literature*, the toll bridge "provides an appropriate metaphor for the crossing-over from childhood to adulthood, . . . and a toll of some kind must be paid."[13] Tess and Jan pay "the eternal toll of friendship," which is "forgiveness of the other's failings" (*Toll*, 196).

Similarly, the raven that visits the toll house is a real bird. Adam is able to coax it down and even talk to it, showing his connection with animals and children (note his affinity with the Downs Syndrome children) and his own innocence and trustworthiness. After Adam's return to his old violent life, at least in his mind (a blow on the head restoring his memory of it), he is unable to call the raven down a second time. Like the albatross around the Ancient Mariner's neck or the white whale in *Moby Dick*, the raven suggests a number of symbolic possibilities. Since ancient times, the raven has been considered a bird of ill omen, symbolic of grief, death, and destruction, associations Shakespeare uses in *Macbeth* and *Othello* and Poe uses in "The Raven." In *The Toll Bridge*, Jan certainly recognizes these associations, commenting that with the raven's predatory appearance it's no wonder it gets such bad press. When the raven comes back day after day, Jan says that he begins to wonder if it was actually calling for Adam. And when Adam brings the raven into the toll house, "In seconds the place looked and smelled like a dungeon in the bowels of hell during an attack from an avenging angel" (*Toll*, 113). Adam, however, seems to be calmed by the raven and the chaos it creates, exhilarated by his close encounter with such a creature. After Adam has been injured, however, and his memory of Aston restored, he fails to coax the raven down a second time and looks now to Jan like "a caged animal," stalking about with "a restless, angry, desperate, defeated, slow, irritating tread" (*Toll*, 224). As Adam, he can calm the raven as it calms him, he is in control, but death and destruction are "calling for him." As Aston, he can't toy with death any longer; he is trapped and hopeless.

Symbol suggests instead of spelling out. Water and fire, silver chains and Janus cups, raven stares and vulpine grins, and above all "an old bridge and an ageless river flowing through the English countryside," as a review in *School Library Journal* points out, these and other symbols "combine to form a metaphor for the journey of self-discovery. . . . "[14]

THE ART OF THE FUGUE

The word *fugue* means to flee. In psychology, a person who has entered the Fugue state, as Adam/Aston has, tries to run away—his doctor says from himself—and forgets his past life. Jan is also running away when he comes to the toll bridge, from himself the way everyone at home defines him, even if he doesn't recognize what he's doing as flight. He *wants* to forget his past life. Tess recognizes their similarity, explaining in part in what way one is a double of the other : "Jan ran to the toll bridge and Adam ran into him there. Two runaways colliding . . ." (*Toll*, 154). In music, a fugue is a complex form in which a theme is first stated, and then repeated and varied with accompanying contrapuntal lines. Two or more musical lines are going on at once, as Bach details in his treatise *The Art of the Fugue*. Just as the title "The Toll Bridge" has more than one meaning, so too does the word "fugue." So too, Chambers tells us, does the human personality. It is always made up of two or more forces.

Chambers calls the reader's attention to these parallels between music and personality as Tess stands looking at the injured Adam for the first time:

What phonemes spoke to her as she stood in the waist of the boat?

Regret: limb-weakening, stomach-sickening
Fright: bowel-loosening, nerve-jangling, sweat-making
Pity: tear-inducing
Disgust: fist-clenching, mouth-twisting
Anger: breath-catching, heart-gripping

And, counterpoint to these negatives, a positive that held them in play as the pulsing rhythm of a harmonic holds discords, the beat of the heart driving the flow of blood, she was also possessed by (God, how words fail us now!)

Joy
Gladness
Exhilaration
Zest

As she endured this, Tess felt as if she were split in two: one part of her suffering regret and guilt and sorrow; the other dispassionate, detached, cool, observing the self who suffered, and taking pleasure in it. (*Toll*, 201–2)

Tess, too, is a part of this fugue, as she also repeats and varies the theme.

The key is to accept the doubleness, the yin and the yang, the kiss of two cones, as a fugue finally resolves its contrapuntal strands, and as Jan learns to integrate the various sides of his personality. "I am Janus," he says, " Dually watchful. Of the other, of myself. Of outer, of inner. Of my him, of my her. Constant ambivalence, happy ambiguity" (*Toll*, 225). The dance continues.

NOTES

1. Chambers, personal interview.
2. Chambers, personal website. Retrieved from www.aidanchambers.co.uk/faqs.htm.
3. Chambers, e-mail correspondence, 16 January 2005.
4. Chambers, personal interview.
5. Chambers, quoted in Alison Brace, "Shock Tactics," *The Guardian* 11 July 2000. Academic Search Premier. 25 January 2004. Keyword: Chambers, Aidan.
6. Aidan Chambers, *The Toll Bridge* (New York: Harper, 1992), 16. Hereafter cited in the text as *Toll*.
7. Chambers, personal interview.
8. Chambers, personal website. Retrieved from www.aidanchambers.co.uk/faqs.htm.
9. Chambers, personal website. Retrieved from www.aidanchambers.co.uk/journalism.htm.
10. Chambers, e-mail correspondence, 17 January 2005.

11. Iris Murdoch, "Against Dryness," *Existentialists and Mystics: Writings on Philosophy and Literature* (London: Chatto & Windus, 1997), 294.

12. Chambers, personal interview.

13. Victor Watson, "Introduction," *Coming of Age in Children's Literature*, eds. Margaret Meek and Victor Watson (London: Continuum, 2003), 37.

14. Margaret Cole, "Review of *The Toll Bridge*," *School Library Journal* (July 1995), 92.

Chapter 6

Dance to the Music of Time: *Postcards from No Man's Land*

Each novel in the Dance Sequence is an investigation of the consciousness of a young person at the turn of the twenty-first century. Each novel is an investigation of a different kind of love. And each novel is an investigation of narrative form. That pattern had defined itself by the time Chambers was to start the fifth novel in the sequence. However, Chambers had to find the story. It was while Chambers was still writing *The Toll Bridge* and was in the Netherlands to promote *NIK: Now I Know* that the story for his next novel came to him, quite suddenly, as the kernels for all the other novels had. As he tells the story, he had gone on his own to eat in a café in Amsterdam, which he normally doesn't like to do, but it was so cold in the apartment where he was staying that he wanted to get warm. He took a book with him, "on the basis that if you're alone in a restaurant you have something to read," although he says he's not really able to attend to it. He took Paul Auster's *The Invention of Solitude*, a book that includes a section about the time when Auster was a teenager (although he calls himself "A," in the same way that Kafka calls himself "K") and went to Amsterdam to see the paintings of Vincent Van Gogh, many of which are collected there in a museum devoted to his work. As Chambers sat in this crowded café, reading about the people all around him, he was struck, he says, by the way a story set in the Netherlands would allow him to bring in features he felt were missing up to that point in his sequence.[1]

He felt that you can't talk about the twentieth century without talking about city life, which the other novels in the sequence didn't do. "I dislike cities so much," he says, "I resisted it." Also, none of the other novels had dealt with history, "and that had to be done somehow." He knew that other aspects of life were missing as well: "I knew that in none of them had I dealt with abroad, or going to a foreign place, literally and in your head. I knew that in none of them had the central character been cut off from immediate family, or home circumstances or culture. And I needed a confrontation with another language." France and Spain wouldn't do, he decided, because most English schoolchildren are taught something about those languages. Germany and Russia had complications from their past histories. And he didn't want to go far. Dutch would be perfect, because "no one is taught Dutch, and the Dutch speak English so fluently." He suddenly remembered that *the* one battle he knew well was the battle of Arnhem in World War II, which took place on Dutch soil when British and American soldiers tried to defeat the Germans there and which happened when Chambers was just ten. "It's a very self-contained battle," he recalled. "You can deal with it easily." He knew right then that, as he recounts, "This is perfect. I've got it all."[2]

The story that began in that Amsterdam café was to become *Postcards from No Man's Land*, a novel that integrates two different stories told in alternating chapters by different narrators. In one strand, which takes place in the present day, seventeen-year-old Jacob Todd, on his own for the first time, travels from his home in England to the Netherlands at his grandmother's request to take part in the fifty-first anniversary commemoration of the Battle of Arnhem, in which his grandfather, also named Jacob, died. He is to stay in Haarlem with the family that took care of his grandfather after he was injured, but because the family is absorbed in its own difficulties involving the terminal illness of the grandmother, he is left very much on his own to explore and get to know nearby Amsterdam, where his favorite author, Anne Frank, wrote her famous diary.

He hates the city at first, where he gets picked up by a boy he mistakes for a girl, mugged, and then lost, in every sense of the word. As he gets to know the city and some of its residents, however, including the son of the family with whom he has come to stay, he learns to love Amsterdam, even deciding that he wants to come back for a longer time and learn the language. This story, told in the third-person, alternates with the first-person journal of Geertrui Wesseling, an old woman now but recounting the time when she was nineteen and with her parents cared for the British and American soldiers who had parachuted into her village in the Netherlands to liberate it from the Nazis. One of those men was Jacob Todd, the grandfather of the boy come to the Netherlands for the commemoration of the Battle of Arnhem, which inspired the movie *A Bridge Too Far*. When Geertrui falls in love with Jacob, the ramifications reverberate down the years, touching even the grandson.

When it was published in 1999, after a difficult and painful ten-year "birth" process, *Postcards from No Man's Land* won Britain's prestigious Carnegie Medal, awarded every year to the most distinguished book for children or young adults, an award often compared to the Newbery Medal in the United States. On its publication in the United States in 2002, it won the Michael L. Printz Award for best young adult novel. The judges on the Carnegie committee, who were in unanimous agreement, described the novel as "exceptional—the kind of book that gives you hope for the future of literature for children and young people. . . . Its greatest strength is that it trusts its readers. . . . It trusts young people to understand things and to make their own choice. . . . *Postcards* offers a reader an experience that is second to none."[3] What the novel offers readers is the opportunity to see the world through the eyes of two young people going through intense rites of passage—of innocence growing to experience. As Chambers notes, "Teenagers are better informed today, but may be none the wiser. You get to be wiser by storying the world and seeing it through other forms of consciousness than your own."[4] Along the way, he provides for readers wise, clear-eyed guides in the form of the writer Anne Frank and the painter Rembrandt van Rijn.

THE DANCE ALMOST STILLED

Postcards from No Man's Land may have won all the major awards, but it was almost abandoned two-thirds of the way through. Chambers struggled with writing it, for at the same time he was struggling with a personal crisis that became a professional one. He explains, "I was approaching 60, and I began to struggle with that, heavily. I really, really did not want to be 60. I really hated that. I fought it all the time." He says that his wife also had a difficult time because he was so deeply depressed. Chambers understands the depressions that his principal characters suffer because he has also suffered from them all his life. Even though he was in the middle of writing the book that was to become *Postcards*, he told his publisher that he was through, not writing anymore. And he gave it up. He says that he felt he hardly knew kids anymore and was afraid he was out of sympathy with them, or with their culture.

He had been booked for over a year to be a writer-in-residence at a university in northern Sweden, and although he dreaded having to talk about his books, he went through with his commitment. Two days before he left England, he received a letter from two fifteen-year-old Swedish girls who wanted to meet with Chambers while he was in their town for a conference. "Well, I won't just say no," he recounts, laughing, "but I'll give them a time that won't do." He told them the only time he would have would be after the conference was over at 6:00 P.M. on a Sunday. When he heard nothing from them, he assumed the meeting would not take place. When he got to the town, however, he was told that there were not two but twenty fifteen- and sixteen-year-olds from two schools who had come to meet him, half who had read *The Toll Bridge* and half who had read *Dance on My Grave*. Chambers was even more reluctant by the time Sunday came because he just wanted to go home (he says that he is a very bad traveler), but he walked up what he says was a "cold, empty, dreadful street, to a café with a red light above the door," to a dark, completely silent room. He continues the story: "I went in—I'll never forget it—they were in a dark room with two big tables, but all were standing in a semi-circle. No boys at all. And there was every kind of Swede: the very tall, blonde, thin ones; the short round ones; and everything in between. Absolutely delightful, all of them, and just standing there grinning. Not a sound, just grinning at me. So I grinned at them. It was like a breath of fresh air. It was lovely."[5]

Since they wouldn't ask questions or talk at all, Chambers had them go around the table, tell their names, and tell one thing they liked about the book they read. But after this they still wouldn't talk, until he said that he was going home, and the first question, *the* one he didn't want, was "What are you writing next?" When Chambers told them he had stopped the book he was writing and wasn't writing anymore, that he felt too old, they were shocked and insistent that he tell them about that book. He agreed, since he wasn't going to write it: "'I'll tell you about it, and you'll see why it can't be done. . . . This is a story set in Amsterdam, which you know nothing about. Half the book is written by an old woman living in Holland who's young in the war, and you know nothing about that. It's got a battle in it that you know nothing about. You've barely heard of the Second World War and wouldn't be interested anyway.' I went on for twenty minutes. And I said, 'There you are. Now you can see why I'm not going to write that book. And in any case, if I were going to write it, it's not a book you'd want to read anyway. It's an adult book.' " A girl sitting opposite Chambers replied, "No, that's not an adult book. Adults won't understand it." He says that he was so shocked that he didn't ask her to explain. He only asked the rest of the group whether they were in agreement. "Oh, yes," they said, "it's perfectly obvious."

Chambers describes what happened next as "very, very weird." The whole atmosphere changed—he says he can feel it now—became extremely, intensely intimate. The girls were in fact inching their chairs closer and closer, saying "No, no, you have to go on and do this. It doesn't matter how old you are." And they started telling Chambers what they had gotten from his work. Four hours later, when they had to break up, the girl who had first written Chambers stood in front of him saying she wouldn't leave until he promised her that he would finish this book. He said he couldn't promise that, but he would promise to take a look at it again when he got back home. And she said, "All right, that's all right if you promise me that," gave Chambers a hug, and left. When he got home he remembered his promise, took the manuscript out, thought it through, and started to write it again from the beginning. Every month after their meeting, he got a postcard saying, "How is *our* book getting along?" As his wife Nancy had rescued *Breaktime*, insisting that Chambers finish it when he had doubts, so, he admits, "These girls rescued that book."[6] It is interesting to note that the concept of postcards found their way into Chambers' novel.

Even after Chambers finished writing *Postcards from No Man's Land*, it had a very difficult time in the publication process, so he was completely taken aback when it won the Carnegie Medal. Significantly, given his observation that there is a shift in his novels toward the female, he talks about *Postcards* as "she": "Since the Carnegie, she's gone everywhere. She's got more translations than any of the others. *Dance on My Grave* had always been the one most read, in every language, and now *Postcards* is matching it, easily. Totally unexpected." A favorite author of Chambers, D. H. Lawrence, remarked, "Never trust the teller. Trust the tale." As this novel's history demonstrates, authors are not always the best judge of their own work.

THE "SHE" IN THE DANCE

At first acquaintance *Postcards from No Man's Land* may seem to be a very masculine book. The soldier Jacob; the young Jacob now; Jacob's host in Amsterdam, Daan, the son of the family who has cared for the grandfather Jacob in the war—these males appear at first to be the focus of the novel. The novel even at first appeared that way to Chambers. He knew that the pattern of the six novels in the Dance Sequence was describing a shift to the female, but he at first couldn't see how this novel fit into that shift. But Chambers refuses to reshape his novels to fit a preconceived pattern. The novel must be what it wants to be, not what Chambers wants it to be. What Chambers says he realized as he contemplated the novel is that while it appears to be about these men, every one of them can only do what they do—can only exist, really—because of all the women around them.

The soldier Jacob is perhaps the most obvious example. In September 1944, young nineteen-year-old Geertrui sees Jacob's group of soldiers parachuting into her village on their way to Arnhem, where a key bridge over the Rhine was to be captured by the Allies so that their main army could cross the river, cut off the German army occupying Holland, and thus end the war. As she hears a group of English soldiers on her doorstep saying how thirsty they are, she runs to get a pitcher of water, though her father, as always, tries to hold her back because he is concerned for her safety. When Jacob first sees her in her doorway, he calls her "an angel of mercy."[7] The battle doesn't go well for the Allies. Geertrui wants to help in the makeshift hospital, but her father forbids it, telling his wife that he doesn't want them to have a childless old age with no one to take care of them. His wife stands up to him, saying "[T]hink of our daughter. Isn't it natural she wants to play her part? When this horror is over, what would you have her say, that she had to stand by and watch while others took all the risks? That when the moment came, she wasn't allowed to help?" (*Postcards*, 21). Mother and daughter have their way and end up caring for Jacob when he is brought back to their house unconscious and severely wounded. As

Geertrui bathes his private parts, she leaves another part of her ignorance, and her childhood, behind. Perhaps because of her newfound maturity she is angrily forthright about announcing *her* decision to stay with Jacob when the rest want to leave him in the village and abandon him to certain death when all his friends retreat, and so she persuades her brother, her brother's friend Dirk, and the wounded Jacob to go with her to the farm of Dirk's parents to hide from the Nazis.

Jacob quite literally wouldn't have survived without Geertrui's care. In addition, it is her point of view and not Jacob's that the reader hears. Beginning with the second chapter of *Postcards*, and in every other chapter called "Geertrui"—roughly half of the novel— the reader hears her telling what happened between her and Jacob fifty years ago. Only gradually do we learn that she is writing in the present, addressing the journal to someone specific. And only gradually do we learn that that someone is the grandson Jacob. Yet, as all the other writers in Chambers' novels, while addressing someone specific outside herself, she is really writing to herself. She realizes this fact when she tries to explain why she writes even about the most intimate details: "[L]ike those tedious holiday-making travelers who turn up to coffee armed with their snapshots, I am impelled to spell it out by some irresistible compulsion. To relive it myself, perhaps? To memorialize something that fixed the rest of my life? To confirm its reality?" (*Postcards*, 196). What happened isn't *real* until she writes it down. She also says later essentially the same thing Tess says in *The Toll Bridge* about Jan's writing: humans have a need to confess (*Postcards*, 255).

Geertrui is only the most obvious example of Chambers' point that *Postcards* is really a book about women and "the saving nature of women."[8] In Geertrui's story of wartime Holland, there is Geertrui's mother, who has already been described, and the mother of Dirk, the farmer's wife the four young people go to in order to hide, who also saves Jacob when she thinks quickly enough to hide him from a group of Nazis come to search their farm. The contrast between these women, including Geertrui, and the boy-men, as Geertrui calls them, is telling, for the males want to compete, show off, almost *enjoy* war, while the women hate everything about it. Geertrui is exasperated with the males for their fascination with guns, their "deathly toys" (*Postcards*, 77), and for their "boy-bluster" (*Postcards*, 146).

The women in the contemporary Jacob's story are similarly nurturing. When Jacob is mugged on his first day in Amsterdam, he is helped by Alma, an older woman who takes him in just as she would take in any young street person, for she argues that she remembers the war when everyone was in it together, not like the present when, even when we have much, we allow children to be homeless. There is the older Jacob's widow, Sarah, who is the younger Jacob's grandmother, with whom he lives because they get on so much better than Jacob does with his father and sister. She is the one who sends him on this errand to the Netherlands, and she is the one who began the tradition of sending her grandson a postcard every week, from the time he was six and learned to read. Sarah is the one who not only nurtures Jacob but who educates him in a way, since the postcard's picture is always something she wants him to know about and the message is a thoughtful quotation of something she has read or heard. The three mothers in the contemporary story—of Jacob, Daan, and Daan's homosexual friend Ton—are all understanding of their sons and forgiving, when the fathers are not. While in Holland Jacob meets a girl, Hille, who helps him grow up, both emotionally and sexually. The pattern extends even to Daan, who is bisexual and sustained by a very feminine boy, Ton, but also by a young woman, Simone. Chambers says that what he came to see is that the whole book has to do with the sustaining nature of the female.[9]

LOVE IS NOT FINITE

The female may be the sustaining one, but female love for the male, or male love for the female, is far from the focus of the novel. Daan expresses the point the reader has seen explored in Chambers' other novels when he tries to explain to Jacob his views on love and his bisexual lifestyle: "Love is not finite. It is not that we each have a limited supply of it that we can only give to one person at a time. Or that we have one kind of love that can only be given to one person in the whole of our lives. It's a ridiculous thing to think so" (*Postcards*, 277). We are not one *self*. A personality is not one thing. We are made up of many different selves, as the psychiatric doctor in *The Toll Bridge* insists. In the same way that personality is a multiplicity, so is love. One kind of love *is* love between two people, as we see in Geertrui's diary as she details her love for her soldier, but the old rigidities about gender do not apply anymore. In exasperation, Daan says as much: "All the stuff about gender. Male, female, queer, bi, feminist, new man, whatever—it's meaningless. . . . We're beyond that now" (*Postcards*, 278). When Jacob complains that most people *aren't* beyond that, Daan says that the only way change happens is to refuse to "live the kind of lie that keeps the old system going. . . . All that really matters to me is the people I love" (*Postcards*, 278). *Postcards from No Man's Land* is Chambers' most direct exploration of gender.

The note is sounded in the first scene when the young Jacob is picked up by a boy he thinks is a girl and receives the message on parting that "Niets in Amsterdam is wat het lijkt" (*Postcards*, 12). Nothing in Amsterdam *is* what it seems. And as he gets to know the contradictions about Amsterdam, Jacob also gets to know himself. He meets up later with that same boy/girl, Ton, and discovers that he is strongly attracted to him/her. But he meets a Dutch girl, Hille, at the battle commemoration, to whom he is also strongly attracted. The ending of the novel is ambiguous. As Chambers says, "[Jacob] is in an ambivalent position by the end. Hille takes him to bed. Ton is asking him back, and he's coming back, so you don't really know how he's going to end up, sexually or in his attitudes."[10] Jacob feels his insides shifting, "the parts of his inner self that inhabited his body," as he tries to come to terms with everything that he's learned. What he is beginning to glimpse is "his self," which is "a number of different beings, different Jacobs, rather than just one" (*Postcards*, 280). But he needs time to sort it all out.

If love is not a matter of gender, and not one thing, what is it? *Postcards'* answer to that question is first suggested by two Rembrandt portraits Jacob sees in Amsterdam's great art museum, one of Rembrandt's son Titus and one of the painter himself. As Jacob looks at these two portraits and listens to Daan tell about the lives of father and son, he comes to agree with Geertrui's definition that love is observing with "complete attention" (*Postcards*, 86), as painter and model do with each other. As all art does, literature as well as the visual arts: "[A]ll art is love, because all art is about looking closely. . . . The artist looking closely while he paints, the viewer looking closely at what has been painted" (*Postcards*, 86). If the history of art is the history of love, as Daan suggests, then love can also be for a thing or a place, for as Jacob observes Holland more and more closely, he comes to like it more and more, then love it.

Jacob's response after he has the embarrassing encounter with the boy/girl and then is mugged by a boy who seems, inexplicably, to encourage and enjoy being chased is "to hate this place" (*Postcards*, 26). However, as he sits on the train going to visit Geertrui in her nursing home, he looks at the landscape "with its wide low sky, softened with haze, so that land and sky almost merged," at the colors that are burnished reds "of old brick and roof tiles" and "fresh shining greens and browns of the strips of field," and at the people "getting on with life without any fuss," and he realizes that he hadn't noticed any of this until now. He thinks to himself with surprise, "For the first time since he arrived he began to like the place" (*Postcards*, 122). When Ton takes him on a tour of Amsterdam in a boat, Jacob sees, really sees it for the first time: "It was like suddenly looking at someone you hadn't taken much notice of before, hadn't even liked, and seeing that he, she, was very attractive" (*Postcards*, 244). Jacob realizes then with a start, "It's just like falling for a person. Not wanting to be parted from it, wanting to know everything about it, liking it as it is, the bad as well as the good, the not so pretty as well as the beautiful, its noises and smells and colors and shapes and oddities. Liking its difference from everywhere else. And its history as well as its present. And its mystery, for there was so much he did not understand" (*Postcards*, 294). Just like himself and the people he comes to care for, Amsterdam is not one thing—it is hermaphroditic, even in its architecture: "Strong upstanding bricky maleness and curving flowing liquidy femaleness" (*Postcards*, 244). If each of the novels in the "Dance Sequence" is about a different kind of love, *Postcards from No Man's Land* is more than anything about love of place.

INNOCENT PROTAGONISTS AND CLEAR-EYED GUIDES

As I have indicated, each novel in the "Dance Sequence" is also an investigation of the consciousness of a young person at the turn of the twenty-first century. Jacob is the traditional innocent abroad at the start of the novel. In fact, when he loses his backpack in the mugging on his first day in Amsterdam, he loses all his possessions—symbolically he is stripped of his past identity. He is also cut off from family. He has to encounter a new language. And as Chambers himself points out, "He meets people all the time telling him how he should behave, what he should do, all that. He's totally innocent."[11]

For example, his grandmother Sarah has pounded it into him that one never goes to a Dutch person's house empty-handed, so he brings flowers for Daan and Alma when he visits. Daan's father goes over and over train timetables with Jacob so he can be at the right place at the right time. Daan even tells him how he ought to behave in love, as we have seen. When Jacob thinks back on his experiences as he is about to leave the city he has grown to love, he calls that first day in Amsterdam when he is stripped of his backpack and rescued by Alma "the last day of his previous life" (*Postcards*, 294). Alma recognizes what has happened to him: "Perhaps you lost some of your childhood innocence" (*Postcards*, 299). *Postcards* has traced that process from innocence to experience.

Jacob is a character in the tradition of Henry James and Mark Twain, authors who also put innocents—usually Americans—in the midst of ancient, experienced, and often corrupting Europe. Such traditions are very important to Chambers. He is often called "experimental," but that label fits only in terms of young adult literature, which has not always used the range of techniques that literature for adults has. As Chambers is quick to point out, all of the techniques he uses in his novels have been used before by adult novelists writing in "the Great Tradition"—D. H. Lawrence, Jane Austen, Virginia Woolf, Thomas Hardy, George Eliot, James Joyce, Laurence Sterne—writers interested in contemporary times, the way life is now. Not fantasy. Not historical novels. But here and now, and how it can be known in the consciousness of man.[12] Although *Postcards* contains historical events, they are being looked at from the point of view of the present.

Innocence extends to both the protagonists in both the strands of the novel. Although Geertrui is an old woman only remembering her innocent past, her story demonstrates not how much contemporary young people have changed but how little. Her confusion, her self-scrutiny, her curiosity, her bravado, all her intensely felt emotions—her innocence—these qualities and more are shared by the young Jacob. Chambers emphasizes these similarities in many ways. For example, the same phrase is uttered by characters living fifty years apart: both the contemporary Alma, the woman who helps Jacob after he is mugged, and Dirk, the World War II soldier, say "Where there's a will there's a way" (*Postcards*, 45, 74). Characters in both stories do the same thing: Geertrui's hand is taken by her soldier Jacob in the same way that the young Jacob's hand is taken by

Hille. Young Jacob even gets confused about which story he is living: he says he feels like his own grandfather married to his grandmother (*Postcards*, 305).

Jacob and Geertrui, then, are innocents, but, also in the tradition, there are some experienced guides to help them find the way. Daan initiates Jacob into the ways of wine as well as into the ways of love. When Jacob suggests, in jest, that Daan is corrupting him, not educating him, Daan says, "Sometimes they're the same, don't you think? . . . You learn something, you aren't innocent anymore" (*Postcards*, 92). Daan is also the one to show him the Rembrandt portraits mentioned earlier and explain why he loves him: "His truthfulness. Always honest. Loves people and loves them just as they are. Never afraid of life as it is" (*Postcards*, 84) Rembrandt is of course known for his ruthlessly honest self-portraits, even as he ages. Honesty, clear-eyed honesty, becomes Jacob's real guide.

Jacob finds one of his guides, also a beacon of clear-eyed honesty, on his own even before he comes to Amsterdam. The spirit of Anne Frank moves through *Postcards*. When Jacob first meets Alma as she helps him after he is mugged, they discuss Anne's diary, which Jacob confesses he practically knows by heart. Just as Daan loves Rembrandt for his honesty, so Jacob loves Anne Frank for the same reason. When Alma asks Jacob what he likes most about Anne, he replies, "Her honesty. About herself. About everybody. She wants to know about everything. And she sees through everything. She's a thinker. . . . And she really knew what she wanted out of life. I wish I had her courage. And I wish I knew myself that well" (*Postcards*, 42–43). Jacob's task throughout the novel is to get to know himself that well and to face life with the same clear-eyed honesty that Anne Frank and Rembrandt did. That is why his dilemma at the end of the novel is so great.

We learn from Geertrui's journal about her complicated past during and just after the war, and Jacob learns it, too, since she gives him her journal to read. They are connected in ways he never imagined. What does he do with this knowledge? The question is not an easy one. Everyone Jacob confides in has a different view about whether he should tell his grandmother, Sarah, the widow of Jacob, and all of their arguments are persuasive. Jacob also knows that his face is an open book, that he immediately gives away anything he tries to conceal, especially to Sarah, with whom he has always shared everything. He feels that she will surely know if he is keeping a secret. He has also had honesty held up to him as the greatest virtue by artists he loves and admires. But would this confession be more for his own sake, to relieve his conscience, than it would be for the sake of his grandmother, who has held her husband up as a paragon all these years and can only be hurt by Geertrui's revelations? As the novel ends, Jacob doesn't know what he will do, nor does the reader. As the Carnegie committee commented, Chambers trusts his readers to make their own choices.

CONTROVERSIAL CHOICES

The Carnegie committee may have been unanimous in its choice, but its choice has been a controversial one. Although the controversy has not centered solely on the "issues" that are dealt with in the novel, many of these are volatile ones, among them euthanasia, adultery, sexual discovery, and homosexuality. Chambers insists, however, that he not be thought of as an "issues writer." He says, "It's not how I see it. I'm not sitting with a list of taboo subjects I'm going to deal with. . . . It never occurs to me that it *will* be controversial."[13] A review of *Postcards* in *Publisher's Weekly* agrees that the presence of issues or "problems" doesn't make this a "problem novel": "These issues never become problems to be solved; rather they are part of the story's texture. . . . No tidy endings here. . . ."[14] The controversy surrounding *Postcards* has been larger than just subject matter, however; it concerns what "popular" literature is and what "quality" literature is, whether these are necessarily distinct, and what kind of literature awards like the Newbery, the Carnegie, and the Printz should be given to.

Journalists have reported what they term a "revolt" in the last few years by young readers about recent award choices. The *Daily Telegraph* (London) wrote in 2003, "Young readers claim that the prestigious contest [Carnegie Award] is increasingly dominated by works reflecting controversial subjects."[15] Even adult critics have been uneasy about some recent choices: *Postcards from No Man's Land* "concerns an old lady, who has decided to opt for euthanasia, recalling her youth in the war, and a boy who discovers transvestite love in Amsterdam. Oh God. . . . It's the kind of thing I usually run a mile from."[16] When considering recent winners of the Printz Award, Patty Campbell succinctly summarizes "the eternal YA tussle . . ."—between quality and popularity, between honesty and protectiveness, between realism and models of morality, between reading pleasure and didactic value—arguing that prize committees ignore these dichotomies at their peril. Campbell concludes by quoting one computer listserv member: "We can disagree about the particular merits of one book over another, and its relative literary quality, but it would be a loss, I think, to give up the struggle to recognize outstanding literature for its own sake."[17] Chambers, himself a lifelong critic of books for young people, agrees that debate about such matters is healthy and thinks award committees should actually publish closely-argued reports about their deliberations, "[n]ot for any reason of accountability, but to contribute to the debate about what constitutes quality in writing, and what marks out children's and youth literature as legitimate and thriving art forms."[18]

A PAS DE DEUX OF FORM

The polarities Campbell points out that are a feature of any discussion of young adult literature are especially significant to a discussion of *Postcards from No Man's Land*, which is a novel of polarities and dualities. In the two stories that make up the novel we have rural and urban, past and present, heterosexuality and homosexuality. We have two families, a Dutch family and an English family. We have a grandfather and grandson, who comes to feel as if he is his own grandfather. These dualities are echoed in the form of the novel, which can best be described as dual narratives, juxtaposed by being presented in alternate chapters. One story is a straightforward love story, set in World War II and told by Geertrui in the first person; the other is the story of Jacob's trip to Amsterdam told in the third person, which, as Chambers comments, "distances the reader from that first-person voice, which would determine it so."[19] Chambers wanted to use a form he felt was "subtler" than his other first-person narratives in dealing with the central thread.

Juxtaposed narratives encourage comparison between the two stories being told. A review in *Commonweal* articulates the effect: "The dual stories in *Postcards* provide rich opportunities for the adolescent reader to entertain certain facts that all of us find hard to acknowledge: that I am not the first person to have thought or felt a particular way; that this reduces neither the intensity nor the importance of my experiences, but rather my sense of aloneness; that my thought, feelings, vocational choices, even the expressions of my most intimate desires are shaped by my era, its values, and its events."[20] The two stories are linked, however, and past and present are woven together—by character (the grandfather Jacob in the story of the past, the grandson Jacob in the story of the present, and Geertrui in both) but also by form. Geertrui's story ends as she gives her journal to Jacob, four chapters before the end of the novel, and Jacob's story takes over. Or rather Jacob's story continues the story begun by Geertrui and his grandfather fifty-one years earlier.

What will he do with the information in Geertrui's journal? Will he develop his relationship with Hille? Will he develop his relationship with Ton? Will he have a relationship with both, as Daan insists is the way out of the old rigid rules for living? Jacob finds no neat answers, as a reviewer notes, "just a sense of the rich and painful confusion of what it means to be human."[21] In those final chapters of the novel, the information presented in Geertrui's journal is always present in Jacob's mind and in his speech, as she is, for he almost obsessively discusses it—with Daan, Daan's mother, Ton, Hille, and Alma. It is clear that Jacob will continue Geertrui's narrative, their parallel lives forever entwining.

LEARNING THE STEPS

In a review of a new biography of Virginia Woolf, an author in the realist tradition in which Aidan Chambers places himself, critic Jane Dunn comments on the way most of Woolf's writing was an exploration of her relationships with others and of her place in the world. "Above all," Dunn writes, "she wrote to explain herself to herself."[22] The same can be said of Chambers and of his protagonists. Chambers admits as much when he writes of his novels, "in every case, even those which seem to be addressed to a specific character, by the end of the book the writer is really addressing him-herself." This is especially true of *Postcards*, he contends. Geertrui quite clearly addresses the contemporary Jacob, but as we have seen she has complicated personal reasons for writing. Contemporary Jacob's story is not addressed to anyone who is identified, yet Chambers believes that there *is* an audience: "My feeling is that he is writing to himself—writing in order to understand himself." Chambers goes on to say that Anne Frank does the same thing for more than half her *Diary*.[23]

It seems as if authors and their characters both write to learn, to gain understanding. And friends, or at least other people, are necessary to help in that process. In fact, that is the way people come close to one another, especially in *Postcards*. As Victor Watson points out in *Coming of Age in Children's Literature*, the characters in *Postcards* are either talkers or writers, for "above everything is the need to tell. . . . This novel is a celebration of people's capacity to make words bring them together in understanding and love—an activity which in Chambers' fiction is central to maturation."[24] Chambers admires all those who write, but he also admires those who read, for that is the road to discovery. In his critical work *Introducing Books to Children*, Chambers explains why these activities are so important: "Always, the attempt in literature when it is at its best is to catch a truth of life, life in its diversity, complexity, familiar strangeness, and to re-create its very texture. And by catching it thus, like a butterfly in a net of words, an author enables himself and others to lay hold of and to contemplate experience, although the experience itself slips away beyond recall even as we live through it" (*Introducing*, 180). *Postcards from No Man's Land* is the best of literature, and it demonstrates how to use literature to learn, about ourselves and others.

NOTES

1. Chambers, personal interview.
2. Chambers, personal interview.
3. Nigel Reynolds, "Falling Under a Different Kind of Spell," *Daily Telegraph*, 7 August 2000.
4. Alison Brace, "Shock Tactics," *The Guardian*, 11 July 2000.
5. Chambers, personal interview.
6. Chambers, personal interview.
7. Aidan Chambers, *Postcards from No Man's Land* (New York: Dutton, 2002), 16. Hereafter cited in the text as *Postcards*.
8. Chambers, personal interview.
9. Chambers, personal interview.
10. Chambers, personal interview.
11. Chambers, personal interview.
12. Chambers, personal interview.
13. Chambers, personal interview.

14. *Publishers Weekly*, 29 April 2002. Retrieved from www.aidanchambers.co.uk/books/postcards.htm.
15. Macer Hall, "Teenage Readers Demand Shift Back to Ripping Yarns," *Daily Telegraph*, 25 May 2003.
16. Melanie McDonagh, "Once Upon a Time, Children's Books Were Looked Down On," *Daily Telegraph*, 13 April 2002.
17. Patty Campbell, "The Sand in the Oyster: Prizes and Paradoxes," *Horn Book* 79.4 (Jul/Aug 2003), 501–6. Academic Search Premier. 25 January 2004. Keyword: Chambers, Aidan.
18. Chambers, "The Death of Populism," on Chambers' personal website. Originally published in *The Bookseller* (14 July 2000).
19. Chambers, personal interview.
20. Daria Donnelly, "This Land Is Your Land," *Commonweal* 130.7 (4 November 2003), 21–23. Academic Search Premier. 25 January 2004. Keyword: Chambers, Aidan.
21. Hazel Rochman, "Review of *Postcards from No Man's Land*," *Booklist* 98 (15 May 2002). Retrieved from http://archive.ala.org/booklist/v98/my2/57chambers.html.
22. Jane Dunn, "Review of *Virginia Woolf: An Inner Life* by Julia Briggs," *Sunday Times* (London), "Culture" section, 27 March 2005, 44.
23. Chambers, personal website. Retrieved from www.aidanchambers.co.uk/faqs.
24. Victor Watson, "Introduction" to *Coming of Age in Children's Literature*, eds. Margaret Meek and Victor Watson (London: Continuum, 2003), 40.

Chapter 7

The Last Waltz:
This Is All: The Pillow Book of Cordelia Kenn

From the time Aidan Chambers was writing *Dance on My Grave*, the second novel in what he came to think of as the "Dance Sequence," he had "intuited"—the word he uses to describe the experience—that there would be six books in that sequence. "It felt like six; I said it at the time," he recalls. However, he never dreamed that he would still be engaged in the writing of those books twenty-five years later. His wife certainly didn't. Chambers laughingly remembers that "she probably thought ten years would do it." Both she and he, at different times, wondered if six books were even possible, whether he could finish them as planned.[1] But the "Dance Sequence" was completed with the 2005 publication of *This Is All: The Pillow Book of Cordelia Kenn*, the sixth and final novel.

As with Chambers' other novels, the subject of this one had to be "found," again his word. He knew that it would be the final one in the sequence, so he had already decided on the title *This Is All*, but the subject didn't come to him until much later, as he was watching a televised showing of British director Peter Greenaway's 1996 film *The Pillow Book*. Chambers recalls, "It sparked a memory that in 1968 I'd bought a copy of the famous thousand-year-old Japanese work of literature on which Greenaway's film is based, *The Pillow Book of Sei Shōnagon*, in an English translation by Ivan Morris. Stimulated by Greenaway's film, I dug the book out and started reading it again for the first time in thirty years. As I did so, I knew I'd found the next novel in the sequence, that it would use the form of the pillow book, that the central character had to be a girl (because the narrative logic of the sequence required it), and that she would be pregnant when she compiled her book."[2] The Greenaway film is one of several late-twentieth-century reworkings of this ancient Japanese form, including books published in the 1990s by British actor Eleanor Bron and Canadian journalist Heather Mallick. Aidan Chambers' novel *This Is All: The Pillow Book of Cordelia Kenn* is further testimony to our modern fascination with this literary form.

The cover of Chambers' novel contains a brief explanation of the form by the translator of *The Pillow Book of Sei Shōnagon*, Ivan Morris: "A notebook or collection of notebooks kept in some accessible but relatively private place, and in which the author would from time to time record impressions, daily events, poems, letters, stories, ideas, descriptions of people, etc."[3] It is called a pillow book because that "relatively private place" was most often the author's pillow. However, the pillow was not like ours, made of foam or feathers, but made of wood like a piece of furniture, u-shaped to hold the head and with drawers at each end. In these drawers the writer, always a woman of the upper classes in the emperor's court during the Heian period in Japan, would put pieces of paper on which observations were written. The word "notebook" really suggests something more formal than the actuality. For example, Sei Shōnagon's work was first published five hundred years after she died, and it exists in many forms—as Chambers explains, some ordered alphabetically according to subject, some ordered chronologically, some ordered thematically—because there was no order or sequence to the original pieces of paper. As amorphous as it is, however, it has captivated readers, who agree with Chambers that "It's a wonderful book, absolutely marvelous."[4]

The pillow book is a very malleable form, one suited to Chambers' intentions in his last book. Sei Shōnagon's work has no real narrative because she isn't telling a story, and Chambers at first thought to do the same thing. As he explains, "I'd been looking for the form of the last book, knowing that it was a girl writing, and I wanted to break away from strict narrative. At first I thought I would follow the Japanese pillow book form and make it a totally amorphous collection of her writing," but he knew that could be tedious in a long book. However, two recollections by Chambers shifted his emphasis somewhat. First, he remembered his experience as a teacher of teenage girls who become pregnant. They all would insist that once they had a baby they were no longer like their friends. As Chambers says, "It does something. It's the end of their youth." He found that an interesting idea, that the birth of a baby meant that you were no longer a teenager, even if you were a teenager. Second, he remembered what Robert Westall, the author of the Carnegie winner *The Machine Gunners*, said about writing that book, which is based on his childhood in World War II. His son was twelve, he was middle-aged, but he knew what it was like to be twelve. How could he share that with his son? Chambers remembers Westall saying that the only way he knew to do that was to write, and so he wrote him a story about his being twelve. Westall called it "my gift to him at the age he had reached. . . . He had shown me how life was for him at twelve and I suddenly felt the need to show him how life had been for me at twelve. I wanted to invite him back into my world and let the two generations, just for a moment, stand side by side in time."[5]

Chambers considered these two facts and decided that if his protagonist were pregnant she would understand that when she had the baby she would no longer be a youth, although she was still a teenager. She also understands that when her daughter is sixteen, she will be in her thirties, and so she decides to collect what she has written from the time she was sixteen with the intention of giving it to her daughter as a sixteenth birthday present. In that way, they could both be sixteen together. And because Cordelia's own mother had died when she was very young, she knows that there are things a daughter wishes to know but which mothers can't or don't usually tell them. Therefore, the book Chambers' protagonist begins to put together has a stronger narrative than the traditional Japanese pillow book because it is *her story*—the story of how she met, lost, and finally married her husband, and how she became pregnant. It is, as she tells the reader on the first page, "a kind of portrait of myself as a teenager." This story is constantly interrupted, however—in pillow book fashion—by lists of things she likes or doesn't like, anecdotes, thoughts, poems she has written, and so on. It is, Cordelia says, "a bit of a hodgepodge, a veggie soup of a book, but it's full of the best ingredients from my own organic garden" (*Pillow*, 3). It is narrative and pillow book in one.

Cordelia is nearly sixteen when she reads that English girls in her time lose their virginity on average at sixteen years, three months. She decides that she isn't going to be average, or after the average, so since she doesn't have a boyfriend she selects one on the basis of what she thinks his qualities should be and determines to have her first sexual experience with him. However, not according to plan, she falls in love with him, but the course of true love never did run smooth, to quote Cordelia's favorite author, William Shakespeare. First her home life is thrown into turmoil when her father marries her aunt, then her emotional life is destroyed when her boyfriend leaves for college and becomes attached to another girl. When she thinks she has lost him forever, Cordelia suffers a number of traumas, both emotional and physical, only surviving because of her growing friendship with her literature teacher and her determination to be a poet. As the back cover of the book says, this is not a novel for younger readers, which is true of all Chambers' novels in this sequence, but the explicit nature of the narrator's descriptions of her sexual experiences makes that caution necessary.

All of this is told—her pregnancy, the birth of her child, and the unexpected aftermath—in six books, corresponding to six phases of her life. There are six books in this novel because there are six novels in the "Dance Sequence"—another example of Chambers' love of patterns. So *This Is All: The Pillow Book of Cordelia Kenn* is a big book. Readers come to know the writer intimately, sometimes infuriatingly. A modern publisher has said about *The Pillow Book of Sei Shōnagon*, "Her style is so eloquent, her observations so skillfully chosen, and her wit so sharp that even the smallest detail she records can attract and hold the attention of any modern reader." The final novel in the "Dance Sequence" attracts, holds, and ultimately moves readers in the same way.

"A PATTERN SO OBVIOUSLY RIGHT"

Every novel in the "Dance Sequence," from *Breaktime* on, has had a literary underpinning, sometimes in folk literature and legends (Robin Hood in *Breaktime*, for example); sometimes in literary archetypes or symbols (the doppelgänger in *The Toll Bridge*, among others); and sometimes in specific literary works (as *Hamlet* and *Henry IV* are used in *Dance on My Grave*). Of course, there are the clear references in *This Is All: The Pillow Book of Cordelia Kenn* to the Japanese literary form the pillow book, but the writer that it owes most to is Shakespeare. As Chambers has done before, he passes along his own interest in language and reading to his protagonist, and so Cordelia's favorite writer—god almost—is Shakespeare, as he is Chambers'. We learn, only at the very end, that she has organized her writing into boxes of different colors, with the title of a Shakespearean play written under each lid, and so each section follows the same pattern: Book One, The Red Pillow Book; Book Two, The Green Pillow Book; and so on. Chambers has gone back to the eighteenth-century tradition of organizing novels into "books," as he points out was his intention.[6] Readers see how the Shakespearean references supply the pattern only in retrospect, after they have almost finished the novel. Each book is different, however, in the way it is told, which continues Chambers' interest in narrative form, as has been evident in all his novels.

Cordelia has written the words "Romeo and Juliet" on the first box. In Book One she falls in love and has her first sexual intercourse, told in detail in the last thirty pages. She and her chosen boyfriend Will are not much older than Shakespeare's two lovers, and Cordelia grudgingly admits a further resemblance. She remembers how scornful she had been of "[a]ll that Romeo and Juliet stuff" before she herself fell in love, but wonders whether it was because "[w]hat you long for the most, you scorn the most" since "in a flash" she "fell passionately in love" and was experiencing "flushes of hot sweats, dizziness of the brain, yearnings of the lips . . . " and other "symptoms of seduction" (*Pillow*, 17–18). There is a strong narrative throughout that first book, a story, but it is constantly being interrupted in pillow book fashion by brief observations, lists, or poems. For example, a description of the debacle that is her first date with Will is interrupted by a list, "Things it helps me to remember," including "When in a bad mood, keep quiet or still," "When you're tired you get doubtful," and "All airplanes go through clouds on their journeys. So do people during theirs" (*Pillow*, 48).

In the second book, everything starts to fall apart. First, her father and her aunt, her mother's sister, tell her they are getting married. She has grown up with both of them, living in both of their houses since her mother died, but suddenly she feels excluded from what had enveloped and cosseted her before. When they tell her, she feels that something "enclosed them in a transparent membrane that I felt I couldn't penetrate" (*Pillow*, 205b). What had been "Dad" and "Doris" before, separate and distinct, has become "D&D." They will sell her father's house and live in her aunt's, so that Cordelia loses her childhood home as well. Meanwhile, her lover, Will, is preparing to leave for college, which throws Cordelia into depression. Chambers writes from direct experience as a teacher: "That often happens to clever, intelligent girls who have boyfriends going away to university. They're just in a mess, because they're convinced he's going to have it off."[7] Cordelia and Will have their first real argument. And he won't tell her that he loves her, because he distrusts that word. *Everything* in Cordelia's life is changing, and she's panicked. She knows that she won't be a child any longer. She is afraid, as she says when apologizing to her father and aunt for her sullen outburst about their marriage, afraid that she is losing everything and everyone that she has loved "the way I've always loved" them (*Pillow*, 305b). She has written on the box that holds these pages "Love's Labours Lost."

This second book splits in its form, the way Cordelia feels she is being split. On the right-hand pages there is a continuous narrative, uninterrupted (these are numbered b), and on the left-hand side there is what you would find in a pillow book—lists, poems, fairy tales, a teacher's comments on an essay, the story from *NIK: Now I Know* of how Julie—a character in this book, Ms Martin now—is injured and how she subsequently loses her belief in Christianity (another loss), and so on (these are numbered a). The reader must decide how to read this section. Chambers reports that the first readers, in his publisher's office, "interleave" it, "according to what they need in their reading pattern of that narrative. They break at different points." That is, they read a bit from one side but then feel "oh, I've got to do that," and so they go back and read some from the other side, and then they go past the part that they read before, and so on.[8]

The third box, The Orange Pillow Book, is labeled "Measure for Measure" by Cordelia. Because she thinks Will is having an affair with a girl at his college, she has an affair with a much older man, her measure for Will's measure. The content of Shakespeare's play also reflects in some way what happens in this period of Cordelia's life, as it concerns a Duke who leaves his rightful place to a womanizer. Book Three is told as a novella, straightforward, with no interruptions in pillow book fashion. At the end of that book, Will comes back and tells her that she was mistaken about him and the girl at college and that he loves Cordelia—the one thing he wouldn't say before and the one thing she wanted him to say—but when she tells him about her "mistake," as she calls it, with the older man, Will does indeed reject her.

The fourth book is the dark night of Cordelia's soul, a black box called "A Winter's Tale," for it is indeed the winter of Cordelia's life.

It is also real winter, the branches turned to bare bones, trees to skeletons. Not only has she *really* lost Will, but she becomes the object of a warped, dark love, as Chambers describes it. This "lover," Cal Bain, is a version of Caliban from *The Tempest* (as his name suggests), the deformed offspring of a witch, called a monster by many characters in the play, but capable of fine speech. He is often referred to as a curious mixture of devil, man, and beast. Chambers says he was fascinated to read Ted Hughes' comments on the play: "Hughes says that the interesting thing about *The Tempest* is that Caliban, who is intent on murdering Prospero and raping his daughter Miranda, is never got rid of. Hughes says that we never get rid of Caliban—we've got Hitler, we've got Stalin, whoever—it's always there, never got rid of. We have to cope with it since we can't kill it." This principle of evil, Cal, is also intent on rape—but out of "warped, neurotic, murderous love" as Chambers describes it—and he, like Caliban, also gets away.[9] There is also an Ariel—Arry in *This Is All*, similar to the "airy sprite" in *The Tempest* who does good. Readers learn this part of the narrative in short scenes scattered throughout Book Four, which is arranged alphabetically like a dictionary according to the first letter of the title of the passage. This book, therefore, is most like a true pillow book.

Book Five, The Yellow Pillow Book, is found in a box with "All's Well That Ends Well" written by Cordelia on its lid. As a result of her harrowing experience in the previous book, there is a reconciliation with Will, who realizes that whatever Cordelia has done he will never be able to live without her. As Chambers says, however, "They're now both damaged people; they're both having to cope with the realities of growing up, of being imperfect."[10] It is written as a short three-scene play, very straightforward, Cordelia describing her life with Will until the time that she conceives the baby.

Cordelia intended to end her pillow book at that point, but when she dies unexpectedly only four months after giving birth, Will is left with this unfinished thing. Cordelia has clearly revised some and put it in the order she wants, but just as clearly she has not revised other parts, which have no order. The goal to complete the pillow book for his daughter is all that holds Will together. Cordelia had left a sixth box, but it contains only fictional works; he and Julie decide not to include this material, and, instead, Will finishes the book as he knows Cordelia intended, with a report of their marriage and naming ceremony. As in all of Chambers' novels, however, the ending is indefinite in that we don't learn the name of the child. How she will grow up we don't know.

Readers experience the shock of Cordelia's death as they do in life. It seems random. But art sees patterns in apparent chaos. Nearing the end she says about some solution to a problem that has been plaguing her, "It was one of those exciting occasions when separate threads that till then have been tangled and untidy are unraveled and examined and then woven into a pattern so obviously right that you wonder why you didn't see it before" (*Pillow*, 723–24). There has been a pattern to Cordelia's life, which her art, in making the pillow book, has woven.

"OUR TIME NOW"

Patterns are essential to Chambers. Another pattern, Julie's icon which she uses to meditate, is on the cover of *This Is All: The Pillow Book of Cordelia Kenn*. It is round so it doesn't matter where one starts to explore its meanings. As Julie says, "everything is related, everything is linked, one thing inevitably leads to another" (*Pillow*, 615). This icon is the spiritual center of the novel, as is Julie. The large pattern that the Dance Sequence has described is an increasing feminism, a movement from male to female, but since everything is linked, readers are left with a circle instead of a straight line. Perhaps now is ying, but there will be yang, or vice versa, as one sector of Julie's icon symbolically expresses the marriage of opposites in that concept of Eastern spirituality. The psychiatrist in *The Toll Bridge* comments that a person's life is not a linear journey from birth point A to death point Z; similarly, when Julie attempts to explain to Cordelia how to meditate by using the icon, how to reach the Silence, she makes a similar comment: "You shouldn't think of it like an ordinary journey from A to Z. It isn't a road that leads from here to there and takes a certain length of time to travel. It's a journey you can make in a split second or it can take years" (*Pillow*, 638). Masculine and feminine are likewise not straight roads, but as Cordelia says to her unborn daughter, "I admit that I wanted you to be a girl. It being our time now" (*Pillow*, 2).

In Book One, in the first section called "You . . . ," Cordelia explains that she is keeping this book of her writings for her unborn daughter ("a garrulous nurse blabbed the news after a scan"). She addresses the baby directly—"I swell with you," "I want to see you"—so her immediate audience is defined. But since a baby can't read, Cordelia also explains her purpose: "I hope we will read it together when you are sixteen and I'm in my late thirties so that we can share the years of our youth, you in the flesh and me in written words, and find out how similar we are and how different" (*Pillow*, 1). As we have seen in *Postcards from No Man's Land*, and as Robert Westall has explained about writing *The Machine Gunners*, the past can speak to the present through writing, they can share experience, which is one important function of reading and writing. Chambers has shown his intense and committed belief in literature as a conduit of vicarious experience in his 1975 essay "Introducing Books to Children: Why Bother?" There he argues, "There are a thousand and one possibilities in life which children quite as much as adults would like to experience but know they cannot by any means that are *emotionally* as well as intellectually affective, except by literature" (*Introducing*, 10). By means of her pillow book, Cordelia's child will be able to share experience with her mother, a uniquely female experience, even if her mother is no longer there.

Yet Cordelia explains something else crucial for the pattern the novels in the "Dance Sequence" have established. She is glad the baby is a girl because, as she says, it's our time now. The shift to the female has become complete. Not only is the narrator a girl, and so is the immediate audience, but females occupy the center of this novel. Cordelia's best friend at the beginning of the novel is Izumi Yoshida, named after the "long-dead but still-alive" Japanese poet (*Pillow*, 19). She introduces Cordelia to *The Pillow Book of Sei Shōnagon*, which starts her keeping her own pillow book, since she doesn't like "stories that go on and on in the same fashion page after page, with no variation" but rather likes those that are like "the English weather and the English landscape, . . . where nothing is anything for long or is ever too much" (*Pillow*, 12–13). She rescues Cordelia's first disastrous date when Will fails to turn up at the appointed time, by coming over and listening and giggling and reminding Cordelia, and the reader, that "it was only to be expected, boys being boys." Cordelia is left with the feeling, as she always is after being with Izumi, "how good it was being together, Izumi and me, closest and best of friends, and our caring for each other and loving each other . . . our laughter and talk and holding on to each other . . . an antidote to the hurt of thoughtless boys and their unreliability and waywardness" (*Pillow*, 36). When

Cordelia is distraught on learning that her father had married her mother on the rebound from her mother's sister, Izumi comes to her again, saying that Cordelia needs "glow time," on this occasion massaging and then writing words on Cordelia's body, as happens in Greenaway's film, finally pressing her own naked body on Cordelia's to "eat" her unhappiness, all Cordelia's words "smudged into silence by the rub of her body" (*Pillow*, 137). Cordelia calls Izumi her "secret sharer," as if they are one.

The importance of women in the novel is emphasized by Cordelia's aunt Doris, her mother's sister whom her father first loved and is now about to marry. She has taken Cordelia in since her mother died when she was five and has provided a second home for her. Cordelia says, "I love Doris dearly. . . . She was the only one who knew everything about me that I knew about myself" (*Pillow*, 14). Doris teaches Cordelia the piano and advises her that the best way to her chosen one's heart is, from what she has heard about him, through his head, i.e., music, and she is right. Cordelia calls her "the guardian of my secrets, confessor of my sins, best comforter in calamity" (*Pillow*, 15). She is sensible, sensitive, and cultured; even when Cordelia has to break away from her, as all teenagers have to move away from their parents (or surrogates), she is an example of the calm caring that is represented by women in the novel.

The love of woman for woman is further emphasized by Cordelia's second "best friend," her teacher Ms Martin, whom readers quickly recognize as Julie from *NIK: Now I Know*. She begins as mentor but soon becomes friend. Cordelia flees to her in suicidal anguish when she feels that she has lost *everything*—her first lover, Will, who is going away to college; her best friend, Izumi, who returns to Japan when her father is transferred; her father and her aunt, who are to be married; her home, which her father has decided to sell; even herself, her confidence. She says, "I could think of no one I trusted, no one to whom I could trust myself, no one I admired, no one I wanted to attend to me, except Ms Martin" (*Pillow*, 418). "Ms Martin" soon becomes "Julie" when she decides that she must trust Cordelia as much as Cordelia has trusted her (*Pillow*, 425). She teaches Cordelia to meditate and she talks with her about her spirituality, which is no longer Christianity, as it was in *NIK: Now I Know*, or any organized religion, but which, as Chambers explains, is Zen: "It isn't said in the book that she's become Zen, but after Cordelia's many traumas she counsels her to strip down, to go back to the essentials and build yourself back up again—your confidence, everything—and the only way to do this is to strip right down. You work hard, you work your way through it, you stick to your schoolwork, I'll help you through."[11] Cordelia comes to understand that whereas she used to have a "girly crush" on Julie, now, as she says, she loves her as a friend and needs her to help navigate. "When I was fifteen, Doris was my reference for truth; now it's Julie" (*Pillow*, 569).

As well as the Japanese women writers so essential to this book (which Chambers explains have defined the form of the pillow book, still often called "women's writing"), many Western women writers play a major role in Cordelia's education. Jane Austen, George Eliot, Emily Dickinson, Sylvia Plath, Iris Murdoch, A. S. Byatt—all are discussed and recommended. Chief among these is Virginia Woolf, Julie's favorite writer, so Cordelia reads *To the Lighthouse*, *Mrs. Dalloway*, and above all *A Room of One's Own*, essential "if you're to understand the underlying thematic nature of her novels" (*Pillow*, 672). In this work, an extended essay based on Woolf's lectures at a woman's college at Cambridge in 1928, Woolf argues that a woman must have money and a room of her own if she is going to write. In many ways, *This Is All: The Pillow Book of Cordelia Kenn* traces Cordelia's progress to becoming the writer Woolf wants. She is "getting there," in Julie's words, but isn't there by the end of the novel. She's figured out, however, that she needs certain things. Even before she becomes pregnant and decides to live with Will in a small trailer, she decides that "a place of my own is essential to me, and always will be" (*Pillow*, 678). She starts learning to drive, so she won't be dependent on others for transportation. She needs a job so that she's earning money on her own. And she needs her writing, as much as she needs Will. At least she now knows what she—what any woman—needs: "I'd outlined to myself and to Will what I had to do to arrange the order of my life so as to protect our life together" (*Pillow*, 763). As Cordelia says at the beginning of the novel to her unborn daughter, it's our time now.

Cordelia even includes a special section in her pillow book called "Woman," in which she rehearses some of the advantages of womanhood, from the trivial to the fundamental. First she discusses clothing and makeup: "I can switch about whenever I feel like it. I can wear a skirt today and jeans tomorrow, and no one minds. . . . I can lash on the makeup or go around as unadorned as a filleted fish. I can wear psychedelic green or flaming crimson or whatever colour

I fancy." She soon proceeds to friendship and sexual issues. "I can walk along with my arm through Izumi's or round her, and kiss her, and dance with her, and no one cares a toss. Try that, if you're a man, with your best male friend. . . . Sexually I can come and come again and again and again for as long and as often as I like (well, potentially, anyway—and with practice and a little bit of help from a friend, I agree). Which man can do that, I'd like to know?"

Cordelia's pillow book disquisition on the female continues through the scientific, historical, and mythical. She is, she says, "the prototype, the first sex . . . the original . . . of which the male is merely a variant." She hypothesizes that that's why men have so often tried to restrict and enslave women: "Because they know the Bible and all such male testaments got it wrong. Adam did not come first. Lilith, the first woman, came first. She came, and spawned Adam in her orgiastic joy. Though, as science has proved, we females do not need to have an orgasm simply to beget a child." She argues from all this that she doesn't want a woman-only world, only that men must "liberate themselves from the oppression they've made for themselves," and "free themselves from their confining taboos, their tongue-tied emotions, . . . and their narrow-mindedness"; otherwise, they will continue to "fail themselves" (*Pillow*, 109–10). Cordelia tempers any too-strident feminism by reminding readers throughout her pillow book that, in the phrase heard first in *Postcards from No Man's Land*, "Where there's a Will there's a way," but here the will is her "Will," or William, sometimes failing but always struggling to be a "new man" and liberate himself along with Cordelia. Chambers says that he has also struggled, but that while writing the six novels in the "Dance Sequence," a shift in perception, in how one understands things and how one looks at the world, has gone on in him.[12] Readers see the results of that shift in this final novel.

"ESSENTIAL THINGS"

As Chambers notes about the title of his novel, one of its meanings is that "this is all you need to know; it's about essentials."[13] "Essential" is one of Chambers' favorite words, and this last novel in the sequence is more than any other about Chambers himself, about those things that Chambers believes are essential. The first and most important is expressed in Cordelia's attitude to writing.

Cordelia doesn't write because she wants to, but because she has to, as Chambers often says about himself. She writes what she calls "Cordelia's Mopes," because she doesn't yet want to claim the name "poetry" for what she does, as Nik also doesn't want to use the word "poem" in that earlier book. But she writes her first poem, and knows she will continue, because she *has* to: "Writing it wasn't an option, something I chose to do, but was a necessity" (*Pillow*, 2). As she considers whether there is such a thing as fate, she decides that "if fate means something inevitable, something required, something that you must do because you cannot escape it, then I know . . . it is my fate to put words on paper" (*Pillow*, 22). She agrees with Julie when she says to her that "you write poems because that's what you *have to do*. You don't feel you have a choice. You're a poet because you can't help writing poems. It's essential to you" (*Pillow*, 554). And after her death Will continues Cordelia's pillow book for their daughter, writing that "your mother loved writing for its own sake and for the pleasure of doing it. She *needed* to write. She used to say that she wrote because she had to and read because she wanted to; that she wrote to live and lived to read" (*Pillow*, 777). For Cordelia, as for Chambers, writing is essential.

When Will tells her something essential about himself—that he loves trees, worships them in fact, wants to devote his life to them—Cordelia confides to him that she feels the same way about words: "I love the appearance of words on a page. I love their shape and the patterns they make. I feel them like pebbles in my mouth, I hear them like music in my head. When I write, they are sculptures in my hand." She concludes, "If I have a creed, this is it: My God is language. And there is no other God but this" (*Pillow*, 76–77). Chambers says the same thing about his own beliefs. In a newspaper interview after he won the Carnegie Medal, he commented, "What I believe now . . . is that language is God. . . . 'In the beginning was the Word.'"[14] In his critical text *Introducing Books to Children*, he quotes the same biblical passage, from St. John, saying that John is "only too right." Much work in education, Chambers points out, is "an endless attempt to help children to learn how to articulate [their] confusion of experiences and so come to grips with it. Without language, the basic and demotic tool, no one would have a chance . . ." (*Introducing*, 3). And similar to what George Orwell argues in "Politics and the English Language," that ugly and corrupted language leads to muddy and foolish thinking, even possibly totalitarianism,

Chambers asserts that "what we can do with ourselves is limited by what we can do with our language" (*Booktalk: Occasional Writing on Literature and Children*, 10).

These reasons why words are important are certainly part of Chambers' argument, but his main argument is articulated by Cordelia when she tries to answer her own question, "When I'm writing in my pillow book . . . , who am I writing to?"

> Am I writing to myself in years to come, when I'm a lot older and have started to forget and need to be reminded of how I used to be? Probably. But that's not all. For I do feel that I'm writing to someone and for someone who is here right now. Perhaps the self who writes is writing to, and writing for, one or more of my other selves. Maybe my readers are my other selves.
>
> Also, maybe the self who is writing is not always the same self, but might be any one of my other selves? This would explain why my writing isn't always the same in style, not always the same in the way I express what I want to say and the things I write about.
>
> The self who is writing each time is the self who needs to say something, and the self who is being written to is the self who needs to read it.
>
> This must be how I tell myself about myself.
>
> This must be how I find out about myself.
>
> This must be why writing is so important to me. (*Pillow*, 202a)

The answer Cordelia comes to is the same one Chambers articulates about all his narrators, that even when there seems to be a specific character within a book to whom it is addressed, the writer is really addressing his or her "other self," in order to understand himself or herself, as Anne Frank does through much of her diary.[15]

To understand oneself, to be conscious, is the highest good for Chambers, and it is the most important goal. Again and again Cordelia says how much she hates not understanding herself and how much she wants to know *everything* about her life, for, she asks, "Is there life, are you alive, if you don't know it? What else is life but *knowing* it? Knowing *is* life" (*Pillow*, 87). For example, she doesn't know what to think about the fact that she looks so much like her mother, then asks herself why she always wants to think something, or understand something. "Why do I want to know so much—No, not *know*. What? Be *aware* of? Be *conscious* of? Yes, that's it (*Pillow*, 135). When she tries to explain to her father and aunt why she was so upset about their marriage, she ends in another outburst about her not understanding: "I just *don't know*—and I *hate*, I really really HATE *not knowing*—because as far as I can see, knowing is everything—there's nothing if you don't *know*—and *knowing* you *know*—understand . . ." (*Pillow*, 305b). Immediately after she writes this she says, "To be a human being, you have to *know*, you have to *be aware*, you have to be *conscious* that you are alive. Human beings are different from all other animals because we *know* we are alive and are human. To be human is to be conscious" (*Pillow*, 306a). "Conscious" is another of Chambers' favorite words.

He uses that word over and over when talking about his own writing activities. Intuition may at first glance appear to be at odds with consciousness. It may at first seem contradictory that at the same time Chambers claims to be an intuitive writer he also claims that, like Cordelia, he hates not knowing, but the two are not at odds so much as they are sequentially necessary to him. That is, Chambers trusts intuition to help him find subjects or characters or scenes. For example, he says that he realized only after he had written a number of scenes in *This Is All* with a character called Ms Martin that she was Julie from *NIK: Now I Know*. He won't try to manipulate a book according to a preconceived plan. *After* that first following of his intuition, however, he must stop, as he says he did with *Breaktime*, and consciously work out what he is doing. "To me, all forms of art are about being more and more conscious of how it's done," he explains:

> My father was a craftsman, a woodworker, and a very skilled one. That isn't a way of life; that's a job. Obviously his job dictates how he lives, how he spends his time, and so on, but it's a craft, a work of great skill. I'm probably much less skilled in what I do than what he did, but it's different for me because my writing is a way of living for me rather than a job. And the way of living is dictated by what the writing requires, which is partly an expression of your nature, obviously. I'm very solitary—I'm not gregarious. I'm monastic, really. I still have in my head that a life is divided into worship, work, and study, and that's how I live, really. So my writing is simply a focus of that engagement. I'm attempting to be more conscious.[16]

Both Chambers and his character Cordelia are attempting to be more conscious, to understand with the brain what goes on first in the heart.

"THIS IS ALL"

Another of the meanings of the title, *This Is All*, suggests Chambers, is "This is all I have to say." As such, his most important points from his interviews and nonfiction and from the novels in the entire sequence are repeated and emphasized here. Readers of this group of novels will recognize many of the statements from previous books. Among these are the following:

1. "I've never, even as a child, felt that I'm only one self, only one person. I've always felt I'm quite a few more than one" (*Pillow*, 5).
2. "Is life ever *that* simple? Is it ever so clear and nothing but happy? That it isn't, at least never for very long, is the sadness of [Chevkov's play *The Seagull*], I suppose. But it can be for a while, from time to time. *And in short measures life may perfect be*" (*Pillow*, 52).
3. "How can you know what you think till you hear what you say?" (*Pillow*, 301b).
4. "Books are essential to me. I cannot live without them because I cannot live without reading" (*Pillow*, 562).
5. "Love means directing yourself towards someone else. It means attending to someone else totally" (*Pillow*, 631).
6. "[Julie] didn't say she lost her faith but that she *gave it up*. . . . She could accept the story of Christ *as a story*. . . . But she also said she never believed the stories were literally true. . . . She had no problem with metaphors. . . . But as she understood it, Christianity required its followers to believe that the stories about God and Christ actually happened and were literally true. And you had to swear you believed this every time you said the Creed during the Mass. And she was no longer prepared to do this" (*Pillow*, 406a–408a).
7. "Once I accept that something is finished I let it go without upset and get on with the next thing. Endings have only the weight of the past in them. But beginnings carry such a weight of decision—this route not that, this choice not that—and such a weight of possibilities that they cause me far more excitement and far more anxiety than giving up something that has had its day" (*Pillow*, 739).

These are all statements by Cordelia, but along with the previous discussions of language and consciousness they also represent Chambers' most fundamental beliefs. This is all he has to say.

That last statement about beginnings and endings applies, of course, to Aidan Chambers' whole life, as his biography has demonstrated. It is especially relevant, however, at this time, when he has recently seen the end of one enormous project, the six novels of the "Dance Sequence." These are novels in which the world is looked at through the consciousness of a teenager. "Now I'm finished with that," he says. He is ready to move on to an equally big project: "I will write in the consciousness of an old man. Because it's a new state. Because in the history of the world, we've never had the sort of older population that we have now. It's a whole new territory, and it needs mapping."[17] It's also a whole new metaphor. The master choreographer will become the master cartographer. That shouldn't surprise us. He has always written, he says, in a no man's land, one in which young people and adults can meet and learn about one another.[18] This dance may have come to an end, but a new one is about to commence, one for which readers will gladly learn the steps.

NOTES

1. Chambers, personal interview.
2. Chambers, e-mail correspondence, 16 January 2005.
3. *This Is All: The Pillow Book of Cordelia Kenn* was made available to me by Aidan Chambers in uncorrected book proof form, to be published by The Bodley Head (London) late in 2005, after my book has gone to press. I have listed page numbers from the proof for quotations, but these are necessarily approximate. Hereafter cited in the text as *Pillow*.
4. Chambers, personal interview.
5. Chambers, personal interview.
6. Chambers, personal interview.
7. Chambers, personal interview.
8. Chambers, personal interview.
9. Chambers, personal interview.
10. Chambers, personal interview.
11. Chambers, personal interview.
12. Chambers, personal interview.
13. Chambers, personal interview.
14. Chambers, *Sunday Telegraph*, 16 July 2000.

15. Chambers, personal website. Retrieved from www.aidanchambers.co.uk/faqs.
16. Chambers, personal interview.
17. Alderdice, 28.
18. Alderdice, 27.

Selected Bibliography

PRIMARY SOURCES

Young Adult Novels

Breaktime. New York: Harper, 1979. (First published in Britain by Bodley Head, 1978; paperback in Britain, Red Fox 2000.)
Cycle Smash. London: Heinemann, 1967.
Dance on My Grave. New York: Harper, 1983. (First published in Britain by Bodley Head, 1982; paperback in Britain, Red Fox 2000.)
Marle. London: Heinemann, 1968.
NIK: Now I Know. New York: Harper, 1988. (First published in Britain by Bodley Head, 1987; paperback in Britain, Red Fox 2000.)
Postcards from No Man's Land. New York: Dutton, 2002. (First published in Britain by Bodley Head, 1999; paperback in Britain, Red Fox 2001, in U.S. Penguin 2004.)
This Is All: The Pillow Book of Cordelia Kenn. London: Bodley Head, 2005.
The Toll Bridge. New York: Harper, 1995. (First published in Britain by Bodley Head, 1992; paperback in Britain, Red Fox 2000.)

Children's Books

The Present Takers. London: Bodley Head, 1983. (U.S. edition Harper, 1983; paperback in Britain, Red Fox 1994.)
Seal Secret. London: Bodley Head, 1980. (U.S. edition Harper 1981; paperback in Britain, Red Fox 1999.)

Plays

Bed Time Story. 2001.
The Car. London: Heinemann Educational Books, 1967.
The Chicken Run. London: Heinemann Educational Books, 1968.
The Dream Cage. London: Heinemann Educational Books, 1982.
Johnny Salter. London: Heinemann Educational Books, 1966.
Only Once. Stroud, England: Line By Line, 1998.

Criticism

Booktalk: Occasional Writing on Literature and Children. New York: Harper, 1985. (First published in Britain by Bodley Head, 1985.)
Introducing Books to Children. London: Heinemann Educational Books, 1973. (2nd revised and enlarged edition Horn Book, 1983.)
Plays, Considered as Literature as Well as Theatre, for Young People from 8–18 to Read and Perform. Stroud, England: Thimble Press, 1981.
Poetry for Children: A "Signal" Bookguide (with Jill Bennett). Stroud, England: Thimble Press, 1984.
The Reading Environment. New York: Stenhouse, 1996. (First published in Britain by Thimble Press, 1991.)
Reading Talk. Stroud, England: Thimble Press, 2001.
The Reluctant Reader. New York: Pergamon, 1969.
Tell Me: Children, Reading & Talk. New York: Stenhouse, 1996. (First published in Britain by Thimble Press, 1993.)

Anthologies

Animal Fair. London: Heinemann, 1979.
Cops and Robbers. London: Kestrel, 1977.
Escapers and War at Sea. London: Macmillan, 1978.
Favorite Ghost Stories. London: Kingfisher, 2002.
Fighters in the Sky. London: Macmillan, 1976.
Flyers and Flying. London: Kestrel, 1976.
Funny Folk: A Book of Comic Tales. London: Heinemann, 1976.
Ghost after Ghost. London: Kestrel, 1982.
Ghost Carnival. London: Heinemann, 1977.
Ghosts. London: Macmillan, 1969.
Ghosts 2. London: Macmillan, 1972.
Ghosts 4. Under pseudonym Malcolm Blacklin. London: Macmillan, 1978.
Ghosts and Hauntings. London: Kestrel, 1973.
Ghosts That Haunt You. London: Macmillan, 1980.
Great British Ghosts. London: Pan Books, 1974.
Great Ghosts of the World. London: Pan Books, 1974.

Haunted Houses. London: Pan Books, 1971.
A Haunt of Ghosts. Also a contributor. New York: Harper, 1987.
Hi-ran-ho! A Picture Book of Verse. New York: Longman, 1971.
In Time to Come: An SF Anthology. London: Macmillan, 1973.
I Want to Get Out: Stories and Poems by Young Writers. London: Macmillan, 1971.
Love All. London: Bodley Head, 1988.
Loving You Loving Me. London: Macmillan, 1980.
Men at War. London: Macmillan, 1977.
More Haunted Houses. London: Pan Books, 1973.
On the Edge. London: Macmillan, 1990.
Out of Time: Stories of the Future. London: Bodley Head, 1984.
A Quiver of Ghosts. London: Bodley Head, 1987.
Shades of Dark. London: Hardy, 1984.
A Sporting Chance: Stories of Winning and Losing. London: Bodley Head, 1985.
World Zero Minus: An SF Anthology. London: Macmillan, 1971.

SECONDARY SOURCES

Articles

Adams, Lauren. "Disorderly Fiction." *Horn Book* 78.5 (2002), 521–29.
Authors and Artists for Young Adults. Vol. 27. Detroit: Gale, 1999.
Campbell, Patty. "The Sand in the Oyster: Prizes and Paradoxes." *Horn Book* 79.4 (2003), 501–6.
Carlsen, Robert G. "Teaching Literature for the Adolescent: A Historical Perspective." *English Journal* (Nov. 1984), 28–30.
Chambers, Aidan. "Aidan Chambers." In *Something About the Author Autobiography Series*. Vol. 12. Detroit: Gale, 1991. 37–55.
Contemporary Literary Criticism. Vol. 35. Detroit: Gale, 1985. 97–101.
Gill, David S. "Aidan Chambers: Monk, Writer, Critic." *ALAN Review* (Fall 1997), 11–12.
Gowar, Mick. "Interview with Aidan Chambers." In *Living Writers: A New Approach to English Novelists*. Eds. Mick Gowar and Dennis Hanley. London: Nelson, 1992. 111–15.
Hipple, Ted. "Aidan Chambers." In *Writers for Young Adults*. Vol. 1. Ed. Ted Hipple. New York: Scribner's, 1997. 219–27.
O'Sullivan, Emer. "Losses and Gains in Translation: Some Remarks on the Translation of Humour in the Books of Aidan Chambers." *Children's Literature* 26 (1998), 185–204.
Reynolds, Kimberley. *Children's Literature in the 1880s and the 1900s*. Plymouth: Northcote House, 1994. 48–58.
Silvey, Anita, ed. *Children's Books and Their Creators*. Boston: Houghton Mifflin, 1995.

St. James Guide to Young Adult Writers, 2nd ed. Detroit: St. James, 1999.
Trites, Roberta. *Disturbing the Universe: Power and Repression in Adolescent Literature*. Iowa City: University of Iowa Press, 2004.
Watson, Victor. "Introduction." *Coming of Age in Children's Literature*. Eds. Margaret Meek and Victor Watson. London: Continuum, 2005. 37–40.
Westwater, Martha. "The Dilemma of Melancholy." In *Giant Despair Meets Hopeful: Kristevan Readings in Adolescent Fiction*. Edmonton: University of Alberta Press, 2000. 91–110.

Book Reviews (Selected)

Books for Keeps, Jan. 1999, Val Randall. Rev. of *Postcards from No Man's Land*, p. 27.
Bulletin of the Center for Children's Books, Sept. 1995, p. 9.
Christian Science Monitor, June 6, 1986.
Commonweal, May 11, 2003, Daria Donnelly, rev. of *Postcards*.
Daily Telegraph, Feb. 13,1999, Tony Bradman. "Stories of War and the Pity of War."
Drama, Winter 1968.
Growing Point, Nov. 1978, Margery Fisher, rev. of *Breaktime*; July 1982, Margery Fisher, rev. of *Dance on My Grave*, p. 3928.
The Hindu, May 1, 2003, Prema Srinivasan, rev. of *Postcards*.
Horn Book, June 1987, p. 307; Jan/Feb 1989, Ethel L. Heins, rev. *NIK: Now I Know*, pp. 76–77.
Lambda Book Report, Feb/Mar 2003, Nancy Garden, rev. of *Postcards*.
Lion and the Unicorn, Winter 1979–1980, Geraldine DeLuca, rev. of *Breaktime*, pp. 125–48.
Magpies, May 1993, Melanie Guile, rev. of *NIK: Now I Know*, p. 33; May 1999, Anne Briggs, rev. of *Postcards from No Man's Land*, pp. 37–38.
New York Times Book Review, April 29, 1979, Richard Yates, rev. of *Breaktime*, p. 30.
Observer, Feb. 1999, rev. of *Postcards from No Man's Land*, p. 15.
Publishers Weekly, June 1995, rev. of *The Toll Bridge*, p. 62; July 2002, Kit Alderdice, rev. of *Postcards*.
School Library Journal, July 1995, p. 92.
Times (London), July 10, 2000, Nicolette Jones, "Why Teeny Minds Are Thinking Big," pp. B18–B19.
Times Educational Supplement, Feb. 19, 1999, Janni Howker, rev. of *Postcards from No Man's Land*, p. 23.
Times Literary Supplement, Oct. 16, 1969; Nov. 23, 1973, rev. of *Introducing Books to Children*; Dec. 1, 1978; July 18, 1980; July 23, 1982; Nov. 26, 1982, David Rees, rev. of *Dance on My Grave*; Sept. 30, 1983; Aug. 16, 1985, Lachlan Mackinnon, rev. of *Booktalk*; April 3, 1987, Colin Greenland, rev. of *NIK: Now I Know*.
Wilson Library Bulletin, May 1988, pp. 78–79.

Index

Adam-Aston (*The Toll Bridge*): in Fugue state, 70–71, 83; name change, 70; raven and, 82–83; relationship with Jan, 71–73, 76, 77–78
All's Well That Ends Well (Shakespeare), 111
allusions, literary, 26–27, 41–43, 78–80
altruism, 22
architectural metaphor, 37–38
Auden, W. H., 41
Austen, Jane, 17
Auster, Paul, 87
autobiography, *Breaktime* as, 16–19, 22–23
awards, 1, 12, 99–100

bad seeds, 19–20
Barry (*Dance on My Grave*): comparison to literary characters, 34–36; relationship with Hal, 36–37, 39–41, 43
beginnings and endings, 1–2, 46–47, 120, 121
Bible stories, 35–36
bibles, personal, 63–64
Bodley Head, 11

The Book of Laughter and Forgetting (Kundera), 49
Booktalk, 11–12
bosom friendships, 3–4, 42, 76–78
Breaktime, 15–29; as autobiography, 16–19; as companion to *Dance on My Grave*, 31, 37–39; compared to *Ulysses*, 24; conception of, 10–11, 15; difficulty of, 26–27; narrative structure, 22–26; themes, 20–22; title's significance, 25–26
"The Bridge" (Kafka), 79–80
bridges, 79–80, 82

Cal Bain (*This Is All*), 111
The Car, 8
Carnegie Medal, 1, 12, 89, 99
Chambers, Aidan: adolescent influences, 4–6, 81; childhood, 2–4; depression, 89–90; future plans, 1, 121; marriage, 9–10; monastic life, 52–53; as publishing partner, 9–10; as speaker, 11–12; as teacher, 6, 7–8, 12, 18–19; writing process, 11–14
Chekhov, Anton, 59
Chicken Run, 8

Conrad, Joseph, 19, 41–42, 71–72
consciousness, writing for, 13, 28, 32, 118–19
controversies, young adult, 99–100
Cordelia (*This Is All: The Pillow Book of Cordelia Kenn*): death of, 111–12; female relationships and, 113–16; phases of life, 108–11; statements of, 120–21; unborn daughter, 112–13; writing as essential to, 116–19
crucifixion, 58–60

Daan (*Postcards from No Man's Land*), 98
Dance on My Grave, 31–47; characters in opposition, 33–36; as companion to *Breaktime*, 31, 37–39; conception of, 31–32; homosexuality in, 35–38; literary allusions in, 33–36, 39–43, 45–46; love in, 36–37; narrative structure, 43–45; Osborne as character in, 5; subtitle's significance, 32–33; summary, 32
"Dance Sequence": conception of, 10–14; female perspective, shift to, 55–57, 73–74, 112–13; patterns of, 87, 108; themes, 68; writing process, 105
detective genre, 57–58
Disturbing the Universe (Trites), 37–38
Ditto (*Breaktime*): autobiographical elements, 18–19; discovering consciousness, 28; journals of, 23–25, 28; name's significance, 26; relationships of, 20–22; Robby as secret sharer to, 19–20
Donne, John, 40
doubles, characterization of: doppelgangers, 42, 58; Izumi as secret sharer, 113–14; oppositions, 33–36, 72–73; Robby as secret sharer, 19–20. *See also* "The Secret Sharer" (Conrad)

education, 11–12, 63–64, 117–18
Eleanor Farjeon Award, 12
elusiveness, 41
endings and beginnings, 1–2, 46–47, 120, 121
essentials, 116–19, 120
evangelicalism, lack of, 52–53

Falstaff (*Henry IV / Henry V*), 34, 43
fathers, 17–18, 20, 21–22, 33–34
female perspective, 55–57, 73–74, 112–16. *See also* women
fiction. *See* literature
film script techniques, 61–62
First Date, 8
Frank, Anne, 12–13, 60, 98
friendships: bosom, 3–4, 42, 76–78; in monastic life, 53; sexual love vs., 59, 76–78; between women, 113–15
"From Writer to Reader: An Author Reads Himself," 22–23
fugue, 70–71, 83–84

Geertrui (*Postcards from No Man's Land*), 92–93, 98
gender exploration, 95
God: as female, 54; as invention, 52; as language, 117; as us, 60–61
The Good Apprentice (Murdoch), 79
graves, dancing on, 40. *See also Dance on My Grave*
guides, experienced, 98

Hal (*Dance on My Grave*): compared to Prince Hal, 33–34; homosexuality of, 35–38; journals of, 32–33; name change, 34; relationship with Barry,

34–37, 39–41, 43; reticence of, 38–39
Hal, Prince, 43
Hans Christian Andersen Award, 1, 12
Hardy, Thomas, 70
Helen (*Breaktime*), 26
Henry IV/Henry V (Shakespeare), 34
Hockney, David, 41
homosexuality, 21, 35–38, 37
honesty, 98–99. *See also* truth
Horn Book, 36

identity, search for. *See* consciousness, writing for; self/selves
illusion, 42
initiation scenes, 42–43
innocents, 96–97
instant replays, 43–45
intercuts, 62
International Board on Books for Young People, 12
International Children's Literature Association, 12
Introducing Books to Children, 17
intuition, 81
The Invention of Solitude (Auster), 87
Izumi (*This Is All*), 113–14

Jacob (grandson in *Postcards from No Man's Land*): dilemma of, 98–99; as innocent, 96–98; writing for understanding, 101–2
Jacob (soldier in *Postcards from No Man's Land*), 93
Jan-Piers (*The Toll Bridge*): intuition of, 81; relationship with Adam, 71–73, 76, 77–78; relationships with women, 73–74, 76–77; significance of name change, 69; as writer, 74–76

Johnny Salter, 8
journals: corrections to, 45; of Geertrui, 93, 98; of Hal, 32; purposes of, 93. *See also* writing
Joyce, James, 18, 23, 43
Julie (*NIK: Now I Know*): returning in *This Is All*, 9, 114; role as perceiver, 55–56; spirituality of, 60, 114–15, 120; wholeness of, 53–55
Jung, Carl, 42–43

Kafka, Franz, 79–80
Kenn, Cordelia. *See* Cordelia (*This Is All: The Pillow Book of Cordelia Kenn*)
Kundera, Milan, 49

language: Chambers' philosophy of, 5–6; God as, 60–61, 117; limitations and possibilities of, 62–63; linguistic techniques, 24–27
Lawrence, D. H., 4–5, 17–18, 23, 77–78
letter writing, 59
Lewis, C. S., 53
linguistic techniques, 24–27
literary techniques. *See* language; narrative structure
literature: allusions to, 26–27, 41–43, 78–80; poetry, 63–64; for sharing experiences, 17, 113; truth and, 13, 16, 23, 27–29; value of, 17, 63–64, 78–80, 102
Lockwood, Nancy, 9, 12
logic vs. intuition, 81
loners, 3–4, 33, 51
love: bosom friendship as, 3–4, 42, 76–78; multiplicity of, 20–22, 94–96; as obsession, 36–37; of place, 96; as religion, 61–62; sex vs. friendship, 59, 76–78

Love's Labours Lost (Shakespeare), 109–10

The Machine Gunners (Westall), 107
male perspective, 57–58, 116
Man and His Symbols (Jung), 42–43
Marion (childhood friend), 2–4
maturation dream, 42–43
Measure for Measure (Shakespeare), 110
meditation, 62–63, 81, 112
memory, 43, 45–46
Michael L. Printz Award, 1, 12, 89, 99–100
A Midsummer's Night Dream (Shakespeare), 80
mirrors, as symbol, 20, 41–42
monastic life, 7–9, 52–53, 81
Mother Night (Vonnegut), 39
motorcycle scenes, 42–43
multiplicity: of love, 20–22, 94–96; of personality, 71, 79, 94, 95
Murdoch, Iris, 79

names of characters: changes in, 34, 68–71; significance of, 26, 49–50, 111, 116
narrative structure: autobiographical novels, 22–23; corrections to journal, 45; detective genres, 57–58; dual narrators, 75–76, 100–1; experiments in, 25, 97; female perspective, shift to, 55–57, 73–74, 112–16; instant replays, 43–45; letters, 58–59; pillow books, 106–12; stockshots, 61–62. *See also* journals
Nik (character in *NIK: Now I Know*): crucifixion of, 58–60; relationships of, 53–55; as soloist, 51–52; spirituality of, 60–63

NIK: Now I Know, 49–65; characterization in, 51–52, 53–55; conception of, 49–50; crucifixion scene, 58–59; female perspective, shift to, 55–57; male perspective, 57–58; narrative structure, 61–63; spirituality in, 9, 50–53, 56–57, 60–61, 63–64; summary, 50–51
Nikelodeons (Niks), 51

obsessive love, 36–37
only children, 3–4, 33, 51, 69
oppositions. *See* yin and yang
Osborn, Jim (character), 33, 38
Osborn, Jim (teacher): influence of, 4–6; as intellectual, 81; Midgely, as portrait of, 16–17; views on literary education, 63–64
Outstanding Literary Criticism award, 12

pain, 37, 53
patterns, 13–14, 97–98, 108, 112
"The Perfume" (Donne), 40
The Philosopher's Pupil (Murdoch), 79
The Pillow Book of Sei Shōnagon (Morris), 105–6, 108. See also *This Is All: The Pillow Book of Cordelia Kenn*
poetry, 63–64
A Portrait of the Artist as a Young Man (Joyce), 18
Postcards from No Man's Land, 87–103; awards, 1, 12; conception of, 87–92; critical reactions, 89, 91–92, 99–100; love in, 94–96; narrative structure, 100–1; summary, 88–89; title's significance, 94; women in, 92–94
pregnancy, 106–7
pretending, 39–40

Printz Award, 1, 12, 89, 99–100
The Problem of Pain (Lewis), 53
psychological development, 68
puns, 26–27
puzzles, 25–27

ravens, 82–83
readers, 8, 90–91, 102
The Reading Environment: How Adults Help Children Enjoy Reading, 12
Reading Talk, 11–12
reality, nature of, 26, 42
religion: Bible stories, 35–36, 60–61; Christian characters, 9, 50–51; evangelicalism, lack of, 52–53; faith, living, 59; love as, 61–62; monastic life, 7–9, 52–53; personal bibles, 63–64; poetry and, 63–64; questioning of, 53–54, 120; skepticism, 52–53. *See also* God
reluctant readers, 8
Rembrandt portraits, 95, 98
Robby (*Breaktime*), 19–20, 26
Romeo and Juliet (Shakespeare), 109
A Room of One's Own (Woolf), 115

satellite writings, 11–12
sea rescue, as symbol, 41–42
The Seagull (Chekhov), 59
"The Secret Sharer" (Conrad), 19, 41–42, 71–72
secret sharers, 19–20, 113–14
self/selves: discovery of, 21–22, 61, 74–75, 101–2; multiplicity of, 71, 79, 94, 95. *See also* consciousness, writing for
settings, 23, 88, 95–96
sexuality: friendship and, 59, 76–78; gender exploration, 95; homosexuality, 21, 35–38, 37, 46; initiation into, 42–43; oppositional depictions of, 37–38; search for identity in, 20–21; in Shakespeare's plays, 46
Shakespeare, William: literary allusions to, 33–34, 42–43, 108–11; themes of, 22, 28, 45–46
Signal magazine, 10
soccer game replays, 43–44
Sons and Lovers (Lawrence), 4–5, 17–18, 23
speaking engagements, 11–12
spirituality. *See* religion
St. John's Gospel, 60–61
story as story, 45
symbols, 41–42, 81–83

taboos, 99
teaching vs. writing, 9–10
Tell Me: Children, Reading, and Talk, 12
The Tempest (Shakespeare), 111
terrorism, 54–55
Tess-Katherine (*The Toll Bridge*): name change, 69–70; as narrator, 73; relationship with Adam, 70, 83–84; relationship with Jan, 69, 76–77
Tess of the D'Urbervilles (Hardy), 70
Thimble Press, 10
This Is All: The Pillow Book of Cordelia Kenn, 105–21; conception of, 105–6; female perspective, 112–16; Julie (from *NIK*) in, 9; narrative structure, 106–7, 108–12; summary, 107–8; title's significance, 106, 116–19, 120
The Toll Bridge: characters' names, significance of, 69–71; conception of, 67–68; doubleness in, 83–84; friendship in, 76–78; influences on, 78–81; intuition in, 81; narrative structure, 73–76;

secret sharers in, 71–73; summary, 68; symbols in, 81–84; title's significance, 79–80, 82

Tom (*NIK: Now I Know*), 50–51, 57–58

Trites, Roberta, 37–38

truth: literature and, 13, 16, 23, 27–29; vs. appearances, 39–40

Ulysses (Joyce), 23, 24, 42, 43

Vonnegut, Kurt, 39–40

"Ways of Telling," 41

Westall, Robert, 107

Westcliff High School for Boys, 6

wholeness, search for, 59–60. *See also* self/selves

A Winter's Tale (Shakespeare), 110–11

women: advantages of, 115–16; friendships between, 113–15; God as female, 54; perspectives of, 55–57, 73–74, 112–16; saving nature of, 92–94

Women in Love (Lawrence), 77–78

Woolf, Virginia, 115

word clusters, 62–63

wrestling scenes, 78

writing: for consciousness, 13, 28, 32, 118–19; for discovery of self/selves, 59–61, 74–75, 101–2, 118; as essential, 116–19; to find patterns, 13–14; as gift, 74–75; intuition and intellectualism in, 81; as religion, 64; to share experiences, 113; teaching and, 9–10. *See also* journals; narrative structure

yin and yang: characters in opposition, 33–36, 72–73; dualities, 100–1; of male and female, 56–57, 112; parallels in, 84; in poetry, 63–64. *See also* self/selves

About the Author

Betty Greenway, professor of English at Youngstown State University, teaches graduate and undergraduate courses in children's and young adult literature. She has written *A Stranger Shore: A Critical Introduction to the Work of Mollie Hunter* (Scarecrow 1998), edited *Twice-Told Children's Tales: The Influence of Childhood Reading on Writers for Adults* (Routledge 2005), and a special issue of the *Children's Literature Association Quarterly* on ecology in children's literature, and published articles on many authors for young adults, including Cynthia Voigt, Chris Crutcher, Farley Mowat, and Dylan Thomas, and on many subjects, including teaching poetry to young people, place in children's literature, modern Robinsonnades, and images of school.

She also directs the Center for the Study of Literature for Young Readers (LYRE) at YSU. A longtime member of the YSU English Festival committee, a program bringing nearly 3000 7th through 12th graders to campus each year, and a member of the newly established Faculty-in-the-Schools program, Dr. Greenway works to bring together literature, criticism, and young readers.